W9-CPP-991

Freda S Warrington again presents a personal story that gives insight into the larger issues of life. In her second book, she focuses on the joys, heartaches and complications of a mother-daughter relationship. She cleverly juxtaposes her point of view in her own engrossing narrative with that of her daughter's, as expressed in annual holiday letters. Rising above sentimentality, Ms. Warrington engages readers to find their own understanding about not only her family relationships, but also in their own.
—Joyce McPeake Robinson, *Ed, D.*

This is a gorgeous, illuminating, even inspiring book. As is often the case in many relationships, the attraction between sunshine and shadow is the seed not so much for change, because people are who they are, but of growth for one or both parties. Here, it is The Mother's. This is a familiar theme: The ever-worried, aspirational mother who struggles to direct The Daughter's development into a child of The Mother's expectations at the expense of her own lived life. Instead, it is a celebration of how inexorably The Mother is drawn away from her attempts to influence and control by The Daughter's stubborn passion to choose her own life. Over time, the Mother can finally abandon her post, surrendering and embracing all that The Daughter teaches through example about acceptance and letting go. The loving, respectful growth of the friendship between mother and daughter only grows more beautiful from there.

The attention to detail in the descriptive passages about the goings on in the farming life as well as the attractions and dangers of that life is vibrant, often poetic, always informing the reader of a life we usually fail to really understand. The ongoing fear, grief and sadness of The Mother regarding The Daughter's illness is apparent. Still The Daughter's deep and abiding understanding of the seasons of life and death, her ability to accept with both tears and joys the nature of the life she has chosen, gives rise to confidence in her strength—strength to cope with her own loss and limitations as she takes each unpredictable day on the farm one at a time, focused on the tending of her world and her own well-lived life.
—Dianne Cooper, *MFT*

TheDaughtersAFarmer Press

LISTEN TO THE LIGHT
The Daughter's A Farmer-A True Story

ISBN 978-1-7322319-0-0
Copyright © 2018 by Freda S. Warrington

www.fredaSwarrington.com

For My Daughter, The Farmer

LISTEN TO THE LIGHT:
The Daughter's a Farmer-a true story

Freda S. Warrington

TheDaughtersAFarmer Press

Contents

Preface

As The Mother who has struggled for decades to be patient and compassionate and to learn a new and improved way of being in the world with The Daughter, I've recently become aware that I have a long way to go.

After approving the simple sepia-toned choice of cover for *Listen To The Light: The Daughter's a Farmer* (Book Two), I noticed a strange V pencil line of a shading in the sky beside The Daughter's weather vane. While not always a detail person, I asked The Daughter if she saw the same strange V.

Once again, The Daughter was forced to educate This Mother. That perfect V, she explained, was the V of migrating geese heading south in their flyway over her farm. THAT was the point of the photo. They know where they're going and know how to get there and they were and are a team. She told me, "We always look up when we hear the squawking geese-chatter to see if anyone is out of line or going the wrong way. It's just something we do automatically. We are witness to the natural V shaped migration…a marvel of intersections of weather, collaboration, instinct and imprinted memory."

As I continue to accept my deficiencies and see more clearly, I am frequently humbled by the smallest details that underscore all that I still don't know about the world in which I live.

I remain grateful for the patience and love of my daughter.

Freda S. Warrington
March, 2018
Sarasota, Florida

Introduction

The brilliant Cynthia Ozick, in her essay, "Imaginary People,"* clearly defines differences in The Writer's inspiration. She mentions both memory and observation with autobiography (memory) seeding inspiration in some cases and ideas (observation) powering the narrative in other cases. Still, Ozick believes that no writer utilizes just memory or ideas exclusively. The completed work instead often ends up a "partnership" of both autobiographical material and ideas. Readers, too, Ozick notes, find their own personal "germs" for understanding their lives through reading others' stories.

In *Listen To The Light: The Daughter's A Farmer*, the showcased idea that a carefully nurtured offspring shoots off in an unforeseen direction is so universal that it's classic.

Should we ever be surprised that children insist on finding their own way or their own truth when this is such a frequent fact of life? Why then do parents pursue dreams for their children when they must know that children, no matter what their talents and strengths, will be setting out on their personal paths?

Do we hope that our children will fulfill our own unrealized expectations or further our causes? Are we so certain that we have all the answers and that we know what is best for our children? Are we control freaks who cannot let go? And, what if we are correct and the direction chosen is a dead end, do we say I told you so and stop loving them? Or, as in the case of this daughter and this mother, might they grow toward mutual understanding and respect for different routes toward a rich life?

While themes may be common and while there are no certain answers, it cannot hurt parents to be reminded that the shepherd's crook is not to corral or capture, but rather, to guide.

Quarrel and Quandry: Essays by Cynthia Ozick, Knopf, 2000

THE DAUGHTER'S A FARMER: A True Story

The Little Shepherdess

The Daughter steadies herself against the wall while slipping into her barn boots to fill water buckets and check on the safety of her flocks of sheep and chickens. Constant surveillance is as natural to her as keeping an eye on a rambunctious toddler or a roiling pot of spaghetti. And while this routine scan is generally uneventful, she's had occasion to chase away coyotes patrolling the outer perimeter of the electric fence as well as nonchalant hawks loitering on posts for the best views. Theresa and her egg-laying colleagues are easy targets for these and other predators.

Not so neatly dissected in The Daughter's path to the barn are leftovers from her barn kitty, Lightning. "Better shovel up the carnage," The Daughter thinks out loud. Her mother will not be pleased when she arrives. Of course, The Mother is not likely to mention the unsightly pile of mouse parts on the walkway, but she'll pick her way past and over the remnants taking a deliberately large step that says it all. "How could this horrid farm life be the choice of any rational human being?" She undoubtedly does not remember her own mother's exasperation as she brought home pepperoni pizza and her insistence on paper plates for that and any other treif coming into her kosher home.

The Mother and The Daughter have repeatedly navigated ideological waters around lifestyle and career choices and remain in a quiet standoff. Studying law, The Mother believes, would have made a lot more sense than the life of a shepherd. Whoever heard of a modern day shepherd except for those Basque anomalies in Central California, their hillside flocks turned out for most of the year and then herded down the mountain to shear or slaughter for their family-style restaurants.

It's hard for The Mother to comprehend that this brilliant daughter of hers wields a BoPeep crook when she could be making significant improvements in the lives of others. Only in her imagination can The Mother take pride in a black robed daughter's wise decisions from the bench.

Once, in an undisciplined moment, The Mother couldn't help herself and spoke out. "I'm tired of watching you slipping backwards down a rabbit hole." Her voice had become slow and deliberate as she said, "You are the spittin' image of your great grandmother... an educated woman in the Great Depression who ended up raising laying hens in the country and trekking into Boston with eggs to sell. A dollar a week for her efforts." The Mother's past worries had created permanent furrows in her brow.

The Daughter wanted to ask her mother then, *"Are you sure this isn't about you and what you want for me? A life that would justify your hard work. I should make you proud but bury myself?"* Instead, The Daughter went silent during the perceived attack. She held back her usual defense from what she saw as the imperious, if not accusatory, words of her mother who just hadn't gotten it even after all these years.

With a brief detente underway The Mother pulls an empty egg carton out of her reusable Trader Joe's shopping bag in order to refill it with fresh eggs.

"Is this really what you want out of life? Can't you think ...?" The Mother cannot summon an appropriately intense word to describe what she means but finally settles on the word *globally*? "Our family is rich with global thinkers, but you, out here in the country... you're looking at wool, mutton and eggs."

Meanwhile, The Mother continues filling her egg carton from the cache in the red wire basket on the counter. Two blue Easter eggs, two greenish, one beige, and one brown. She steps back for a moment and The Daughter wonders if her mother might be admiring those colorful fresh eggs.

As she often does, The Daughter looks out her windows toward the nearly 360 degree views, views which comfort and remind her why she has created this place and populated it with sheds, sheep, horses, chickens and gardens. It has taken longer than a Genesis week, but to her mind the farm is godlike in its beauty and fulfills her personal vision. While not perfect, it's what she loves.

The Daughter often holds onto her defensive words so as not to engage her mother in an argument, but she thinks, "*My great grandmother was a productive human being. She put milk on the table for her children and bought more chicken feed. Like Gepetto who labored lovingly to create his boy, that Jewish Bubbie worked with integrity. And no one starved on her watch.*"

The Mother usually interjects a metaphorical verbal pinch thinking she's softening her critical view on The Daughter's choice of profession. "You know I only want the best for you. You haven't got enough strength for this life." An audible sigh was and is her preferred punctuation.

Those were her words several years ago and nothing much has changed. The Mother repeats her sermon. "You're not making your life easier being chained to this place." She sweeps her hands upward in a supplicating gesture of frustration. "You're an economist and a good math teacher. So, what's wrong with a safe classroom and a future pension instead of this zoo?"

The Daughter is distracted for the moment before she realizes she hasn't yet swept the black fly carcasses or scrubbed the dog slobber from her windowsills.

ↅ

In the pole barn with its black iron gates and shiny brass fittings, The Mother sits on a hay bale close to the swishing tail of one of The Daughter's pampered horses with his name plate on his very own stall. "Needy beasts," is the most appropriate epithet she can muster.

The Daughter is patient. "Doesn't it mean anything to you, Mother, that I love this property and I love my life out here?" She gestures toward the front pastures with her sheep and the grazing horses. "Those animals are more satisfying to me than most of the people I know who bitch about everything. I shake the feed pan and they all come running. It's just that basic."

She shakes an imaginary bucket of grain. "How simple. How honest." The Daughter's words trail off into the hay bales stacked to the barn roof as she steels herself to hear the response that is sure to come.

The Mother assumes her daughter's "bitch" comment was designed to sting but she stays focused. "Our whole family has been on a mission to make a difference in the world. Computers. Medicine. Municipal finance to rebuild the nation's crumbling infrastructure. Even Grandpa in the drugstore clamped down on his dearest friend, a codeine addict. He told her, 'Enough's enough!'"

"I'm not denying them their rightful place in this sunny world," The Daughter says. "…but *they* didn't mind hiring out their lives."

"That's hardly fair. Not everyone has cleats fit to their boots half the year to navigate the hills in your side pastures."

"But you love my fresh eggs, Mother, and that makes a difference to you… and to me." The Daughter looks sideways at her mother to see if there's a glimmer of agreement.

"So you benefit when I cook up a warm mash for my "girls" in the freezing cold and when I drag out hay bales to protect them from the wind."

The Daughter pays it forward and "her girls" reciprocate with more eggs than she and her mother can enjoy.

"Well…" The Mother begins but The Daughter interrupts.

"You're absolutely right about our family. They all work hard. But they go to the Islands in the winter and shop at The Green Earth," The Daughter says. "That's their choice, but it's not mine."

The Daughter doesn't mention sanctimonious people she knows who believe they're sufficiently green because they have a charge card at The Green Earth. She also doesn't cite details of the barbarism she believes is inherent in industrial food production or the explosion of children's summer farm camps where parents pay top dollar so their children can touch nature. She doesn't mention that she knows many adults who celebrate at the height of their careers and buy a farm just so they can taste what she enjoys every day.

Perhaps The Mother is a generation behind and harbors the mindset of those immigrants who desperately tried to prove their worth. The Daughter believes she is the one who has "evolved" like the nobles of olden days who aspired to country estates rather than an urban rat race.

ଔ

The Mother doesn't respond as she recalls the nearly buried facts of her own journey whose mission was to stay put and smile in her harvest gold kitchen and, of course, to dream. She hadn't recognized it at the time because she felt guilty about feeling slightly victimized. No, not slightly. There were times she felt pulled under by quicksand and silenced her screams for a flat board so she could crawl on and float out.

She was comforted that she fit the bill for those days. The good wife, the good daughter and the good mother. What set her a notch below five star was her inability to create a flaky pie crust with ice water and her willingness to consider mayhem when her son was paddled by the vice-principal without her written permission.

But this daughter of hers is incorrigible and always has been. A moment of doubt creeps in along with the image of pastel eggs in a red wire basket, and for the first time The Mother considers that she might be the incorrigible one. She's the one who subscribes, and blindly so, to the nurture over nature dogma of her generation. She's the one who believes any hardworking and determined individual can be or do anything. In America a haberdasher can become President of the United States. A regular housewife from Milwaukee can become a Prime Minister or an abused black kid, dressed in a potato sackcloth dress, can become Oprah Winfrey.

It is said that Golda worked with vigor in the Kibbutz chicken coops and cherished memories of her labor on the land.

Still, maybe she should stop blaming The Daughter for what might be an accidental nick on a family chromosome, a pre-determination gene that drew her grandmother's generation to settle in Palestine and farm the land. Survival skills may have been woven even then into the family genetics thereby holding the key for the hyper-vigilance necessary to know when to disappear under floorboards during a pogrom or to note which official was open to a whiskey bribe simply for altering a person's family name.*

The Jewish settlers from The Mother's family who managed to get to the Promised Land spoke eight languages and played chess in the moonlight and figured out how to set an orchard. Those hardy pioneers picked stones out of fields, laid tiles to drain the land, drove countless fenceposts, planted olive and cherry trees and thought

---

*The Mother's great great uncles were Kagan, Karelitz, and Cohen and all brothers. Each was noted officially as an only son and thus exempted from serving in the front lines of the Russian army where one after another would likely have met certain death.

about tomorrow's hike to explore some Biblical spot. Like her daughter, they were imbued with the energy to create a safe place of their own as they sang and danced around evening campfires and set bonfires of thorns for their fantasias. This was no inclination but a strong determination to construct physical independence after history taught this people that intellect and ingenuity was no guarantee for safety.

The fervor apparently skipped a few generations and manifested itself in her daughter.

The Mother promises herself she'll make an effort to read the socio-biologists to see if they mention the futility of attempts to talk sense into a daughter if it were to contradict an apparent natural tendency. If The Daughter's love of the land, the animals and farming is imprinted as surely as is a shy gene, an altruistic gene, or an alcohol gene, and if it insists on expression in spite of The Daughter's declining strength, The Mother will agree to be silent.

In spite of her years of inattention at the little Sylvia Street shul, The Mother often hears the words of the rabbi's closing benediction. Out of nowhere it springs into her consciousness like a musical earworm. *May God turn his face unto you and bestow upon you peace.*

The Mother's silence on the matter would likely offer peace to both of them. But for now, this conversation, as is customary, goes nowhere and both The Daughter and The Mother retreat into their safe corners.

੪

The Daughter, her mother's one and only, cares nothing for jewelry, new cars, designer clothes, or the latest mobile device. She's not tethered to her computer and her smart phone functions mostly as a means of tracking her children. Instead, The Daughter values a simple staff with a generous hook, a fence charger that won't explode every time a bolt of lightning comes close, a reliable golf cart for transfer of muck buckets to compost, and cool sunny, but not too dry, weather for her vegetable garden. She focuses her attention on breeding a stock of friendly sheep from sturdy mothers with marketable wool, good mothering skills and, most important, parasite resistant genetics. These easy keepers for farmers like her are named rather than numbered and spared the freezer.

Her young family along with her farm requires daily attention to detail. All pieces of a clean and freshly ironed uniform for each of her three children including gym shoes, math homework, soccer shin guards, skintight volleyball spandex, water bottles, lacrosse sticks, wrestling shorts and permission slips…algebra, calculus and geometry homework must be ready to go out the door before sunrise minus the memory of the previous evening's meltdowns.

Unlike chores on her farm that are mostly a pleasure, The Daughter is exhausted by orthodontist visits for braces checks and lost retainers, dental cleanings, immunizations and music lessons. Those random disruptions of plans by fevers, vomiting, colds, Nor'easters and blizzards, while adding a dimension of chaos to The Daughter's days, sometimes morph into welcome respite.

According to The Mother, her daughter manages to squeeze in time for her children. According to The Daughter, she manages

to squeeze in time for her farm. Both mother and daughter agree, however, that she's always been different from her high school friends who yearned for designer clothes, football players, mosh pits, jello poppers…and catching a margarita buzz in Mexico.

Cool As A Cucumber

Although she prefers shadow to limelight, The Daughter's not afraid of anyone and at the age of 15 created a momentary ruckus when she quit softball with panache after parental politics interfered with her personal sense of right and wrong. In the game prior to her demotion to second string, with runners on first and second, a line drive flew above her at third. She reached high while hopping backwards to snag it, tagged up, and threw a perfect line to first to accomplish a double play with the parents and kids screaming her name. That was simple competence. But, it was nothing compared to the spectacular grand jete over the cocky second baseman whose face was in the dirt as she followed her coach's order to tag low. The Daughter's surprise leap landed her dead center on top of the bag in a graceful arabesque. And framed by a halo of chalk dust, it was as if she'd descended from heaven. The grinning umpire flung out his arms having never seen that particular tactic outside of a theater.

The downgrade to second string occurred in spite of her error free first half of the season. Disappointed and provoked by the coach's decision, The Daughter let loose an unrehearsed monologue while facing the coach in his office. It was a calm and measured invective in which she pointed out his dishonesty, his pathetic kowtowing to the softball board president who wanted *his* daughter on third base, his ethical cowardice, and his substandard role modeling for his team. She told him his behavior was the antithesis of all the qualities he should be encouraging among her teammates.

The stunning criticism left him speechless as he watched her march off to the locker room to collect her belongings.

∞

The Daughter was even less successful managing her college allowance than her softball career and by November of her freshman

year she'd blown through her cash allotment for the year. She told The Mother, "My bank account is slightly somehow almost empty and the big city is really expensive and I'm only eating one meal a day and some noodles."

Her hint at "hungry" triggered serious sympathy.

"What happened to your meal ticket?"

"I cashed it in because I can eat cheaper at Tom's or Ollie's."

"Really?" The Mother said, "What about your midnight forays to the jazz club?" She'd accidentally received The Daughter's bill in the mail.

The Daughter needed a cash subsidy and fast but hated to confess to The Mother that she was penniless. Instead, with humility she asked the local jeans store for part time work where she learned to size up each customer perfectly, a simple skill to reduce folding time. With similar vigilance, she noticed another employee receiving more money for folding the same number of pairs of jeans. Her demand for equal pay was met and she continued fitting and folding for several months before resolving to pay closer attention to next year's budget.

After two and a half years on the Ivy League campus, The Daughter had learned a lot about herself and the big city as she tried to absorb scarce winter sunlight at her 13th floor open window. The crisp air carrying a faint smell of smoke from someone disobeying the City's burn rules, car exhaust, along with the sounds of gunshots coming from the steps of the classical building at the heart of the campus, were not difficult to integrate into her college life. This assigned room with a view to the neighboring dormitory offered one anonymous vignette per window and dared voyeurs with telescopes to spy on immodest residents partying, studying, showering and, most often, without a privacy shade. And taunting her below was the wrought iron fence where it was rumored a student had recently impaled himself in a bold suicide leap.

In spite of the darkness of her dimly lit room and the drear of winter, The Daughter persevered in her studies even after a car shot through the plate glass window at Ollie's Noodle Shop and landed within a few feet of her bowl of ramen.  Like hooded reapers, unexpected dangers lurked all over the City and at times edged too close for comfort. Whoever would have thought the angel of death would make an appearance at a noodle shop.

After losing her taste for noodles, The Daughter was laid low by an odd cluster of symptoms: a crooked smile, speech disruptions, and one hand that couldn't grasp a pencil. But she practiced her smile in front of the mirror and took her graduate exams anyway using her other hand. But soon it was it was necessary to get to the emergency room of a large city hospital.

Her parents were terrified and raced to her bedside where she lay in intensive care at the local hospital.

The Daughter was unable to speak upon admission. Days turned into weeks with no clear diagnosis. Only her roommate was sure she wouldn't die and defiantly asked, "If you die, can I have your TV?" The Mother overheard the macabre question and did not think it was funny.

After two months of physical therapy, The Daughter recalled how she refused an ambulance so she could drag herself to the emergency room on her own steam. The admitting physician at that time, a former valedictorian of his high school class, asked her, "Do you think that maybe you've been under too much stress? Might you be taking your courses too seriously? How much sleep are you getting?" He finished checking her blood pressure and called in the phlebotomist.

"Your blood pressure is exceptionally low. Do you ever feel faint?" The young doctor spoke in halting segmented syllables as if she were of diminished intelligence.

The Daughter was unable to answer except in a garbled sentence and then decided not to bother.

At the time The Mother tried to convince her daughter to come home where she could recover from this awful malady that had doctors arguing and administering further invasive testing. She offered her favorite foods, her old car to drive, and everything she could think of to entice her home. But no matter how good a case The Mother made, she was talked down by The Daughter, who all by herself and alone, was discharged from the hospital and eventually regained the stamina required to live and study in the big city.

The Daughter embraced the challenge of remaining on campus in her dorm room even after being slimed not only by the shower curtain in the co-ed bathroom but by paroxysms from her in-room sink. That discolored ceramic mini bowl with its separate taps for hot and cold water occasionally suffered spontaneous exorcisms that required The Daughter to dodge projectile insults of grime shooting up and over its edge. So, she responded by stuffing the opening with steel wool and dared any living organism to infiltrate her personal space.

In her easy style, she found hilarity in the battle. With her large worldview she refused to take the attack personally and labeled it simply, "man against beast."

A Horse of a Different Color

Still in good humor after completing her undergraduate studies, she headed west toward graduate school and the beaches of California where she and her new roommates battled plus sized Pacific Coast vermin using rat traps and rubber mallets. Meanwhile, among the jumble of graphs, econometric indexes and equations, The Daughter was awarded two higher degrees. It was during those years, she zeroed in on the right path for her personal zeitgeist, and a lifestyle she believed would contribute best to her health and wellbeing.

At that time, in spite of her eyes acting up, the doctor told her she had 20/20 vision. She accepted that her brain was playing tricks from too many vibes from bored college students signing up for her sections of micro and macro economics when they really wanted to be riding the waves. But a consult appointment at the local clinic told her she had a case of optic neuritis.

cs

Capitalizing on the cool stubborn streak she'd inherited from her paternal grandfather whose fast pitch could have struck out Babe Ruth, The Daughter tied up her sun-bleached blond hair and with enthusiasm proceeded to create an accurate incarnation of her vision of the bucolic life. Her new husband agreed to come along on her journey with the promise of clean air, gardens of pesticide free delights, baskets of happy eggs, antibiotic free meat, and an altogether uncluttered life.

No matter how her family or friends tried to dissuade her from taking on what they assumed was a wink-wink sustainable existence, she refused to reverse direction or change her plan simply because future good health had become less certain. No matter. She countered that no one in this world can predict with certainty the timing of her own future. While no one disputed the inevitability of being enveloped in darkness, she pointed out that individual timetables are not set in stone.

The Daughter threw open the throttle to move at her own designated speed. She and her husband, unafraid of risk, bought the acreage from an old farm and went to work creating their own space that fulfilled her longtime grand wish for a compost pile.

Down to Earth

The Mother describes her Daughter as "feisty," a descriptive word in this case that tilts toward the pejorative. The Daughter considers herself a pragmatist with simple goals that to The Mother are alarmingly empty of merit. The Daughter refuses to believe it's outrageous to want to breathe clean country air or to relish eating a high quality egg with a solid shell and an orange yolk that tastes like an old fashioned egg. Neither does she believe it's odd to attempt purposefully the creation of serenity, her personal prerequisite for mindful living.

The Daughter's plan is hardly original. Mens sana in corpore sano. Plato. Core curriculum from undergraduate days in the City. It makes perfect sense especially after emerging from the underground subways to the soot and sounds of the big city. Who needs the Hamptons, The Daughter asks herself, in order to capture a lifestyle of sunshine, quality air and clean food to co-exist with a healthy mind and brain? And perhaps, if she's lucky, a healthy body? Surely, this unremarkable combination will provide the medium for the best chance to live out her life without drama, hyperbole or hysteria.

The Daughter's contrarian streak is nothing new but within an extended family that prides itself on climbing corporate and academic ladders, it's an anomaly that leaves The Mother apologetic. While cousins auditioned for

Julliard or composed cadenzas, The Daughter was galloping her appaloosa around barrels and leaping hay bales with abandon. With her gang of strong thighed horsy friends, she would lean into her gelding and lope to the edge of the woods and then disappear among the trees.

The Mother's mantra in those days was, "If you'd keep your bedroom as neat as your tack room…" or, "if you can hang up your bridles, brushes and bits, why can't you bend over to pick up your wet towel?"

Racks against the tack room walls supported The Daughter's deep-seated and ornately tooled rodeo saddle and a well-oiled English saddle. On the double row of shelves sat a bucket of alfalfa cubes, hoof polish, buckets of bran and vitamins, and stacked on the floor were bales of hay. Miscellaneous necessities such as overreach boots, picks, clippers, ribbons and rubber bands for braiding a tail or mane were tossed into a giant bread basket pilfered from home. On top of an old kitchen chair with a torn red naugahyde seat rested a rake and a pointed shovel. And the empty wheelbarrow leaning against the far wall was poised to transfer the stall muckings to the unmistakably pungent hot mound composting behind the stable.

This accidental montage, as unpleasant as it was to The Mother, was a setup for a natural photographic still life. To her mind there was little comfort in that tack room beset as it was with flies and the smell of dirt, acidic pine bark shavings, and the fresh manure that made for shallow breathing. That such a place was a precious haven for her daughter, a world away from her demands, made her flush with shame. It must be the space where a young woman could forget about Kabelevsky, algebra, SAT vocabulary and a Jewish mother's designs.

Reaping What You Sow

Now grown and married with three children, The Daughter's plans are straightforward and, in the world of the new millennium with its dedication to sustainability, perhaps noble. Although not without complications, she's certain the farm life is worth the effort not only for her quality of life but to appease the temperamental goddess of good health. With Hygeia but a minor deity, it's clear that those Greeks had it all wrong. What could be more important than a healthy body?

She's delighted by teaching moments that appear spontaneously. Whenever and wherever they land, her children learn about unintended consequences and chickens coming home to roost. They become self-reliant and experience the satisfying exhaustion of hard work. They become partners in the process and don't expect to be paid. The Daughter believes that the idea of living off the land, growing food and deriving pleasure from co-existing with the environment, may be rubbing off on the children.

The Daughter has a hint of suspicion that the same view may be gaining traction with her mother as well. The evidence? (A) Her mother finds those freshly laid eggs irresistible. (B) She's addicted to twisting off and then popping sugar snap peas straight from the vine into her mouth while slapping at the tickles on her ankles. (C) Although not yet a fan of watching the beans grow, The Mother sometimes sits very still to listen to the hum of insects. (D) She breathes in the distinctive smells of the hay or lilacs and does not appear to be offended.

In spite of the trace of give she senses, The Daughter understands it may be impossible to get the approval she'd like from her mother, not a blessing, but just a little understanding.

൯

One step forward but two steps back. When The Mother complains that her hair is falling out, The Daughter thinks she's comforting her by reminding her that the horses, cats, and dogs are also shedding their summer coats as the nights are cooler and the days shorter.

"Suddenly I'm one of your farm animals?"

"No, Mother dear, but you happen to be a mammal and it won't kill you to admit it," The Daughter says. "Like all other mammals, you just may be subject to the laws of nature." She's made her point.

"Do I leave piles of crap all over the place? Were you born two toes and a nose first?" The Mother thinks, *There she goes…explaining everything by the rules of nature.*" The Mother shakes her head. "*A mammal, for godsakes?*" She says nothing more because as usual the conversation arrives at a dead end.

While her mother may or may not be a lost cause, The Daughter sees a Sisyphean struggle in convincing her children to engage in a life close to nature. They want to know why they have to help with the distribution of twenty yards of mulch on Easter Sunday after downing a mountain of jellybeans. They don't care much about some future cornucopian harvest, so The Daughter can only hope for a wow moment in their futures when lessons translate to the real world. Maybe they'll recall with a touch of nostalgia the digging of endless rows of boring holes then dropping in one lovely dried sheep poop per hole along with the seeds for zucchini, blue pumpkins, yellow squash, or chard. Might they understand that the exercise was no hoax?

For now the younger children believe the canard that those carefully planted jellybeans can grow into lollipops by the next morning beating out Jack's beanstalk by a mile.

While seeding values in the children is one thing, The Daughter considers resolving today's dilemma of the barn kitties more pressing. How can she, the protector of the natural order of the jungle a la

Henri Rousseau, morph into a spoiler to ruin a child's Christmas present? What soft and sweet choice of words might she murmur to warn the children about those cutie felines, Lightning and Cloud? "Get ready, Kids. Your kitties will soon be chasing and capturing, along with mice pests, adorable bunnies and helpless baby birds. But don't worry…they'll spit out their legs and beaks." Or, "those bunnies scream loud when they're being eaten." Is that what she should tell her children? And worse, what kind of a warning might soften the blow when one of those kitties is itself captured and eaten by a coyote, a fisher or some other creature? That's one nasty reality-show visual for kids who peel common houseflies off flypaper.

Maybe she can soften the rhetoric with a gentle caveat. "When you beg Santa to bring you some barn kitties, you'd better steel yourself to witness the often cruel cycle of nature itself."

Her mother has always warned her to be careful what she wished for.

Something The Cat Dragged In

The Daughter has faith that her children will use all of their farm knowledge, good and bad, in more valuable ways than distinguishing ragweed from a tomato plant or a ewe from a ram. Instead of choosing pumpkins from a commercial patch, they may decide to nurture their own pumpkins and thereby exercise special care when carving them. They may forever be empowered to fix things, temporize, and extricate themselves from difficult situations. They'll be capable of landscaping, plowing, digging, and harvesting without thoughts of a participation trophy. They may pick up a thimble when necessary to stitch on a loose button.

The Daughter already notices her children zeroing in on solutions to problems like steps in an algebraic equation. If it takes twenty-five 40 pound bales of hay to keep a ewe over the winter, and knowing there's a total of only 400 bales of hay in one 10 acre field, how many sheep and lambs can be supported without trips to the feed store? How high can you stack the bales in the barn without risking a life threatening crash? If the storm cell is moving at 15 miles an hour, will you have time to get the sheep safely into the barn? If one fencepost droops to an angle of 45 degrees because the posthole isn't deep enough, and the fence then tugs the next posts to more acute geometric angles, will the rams be able to hop the fence to find girlfriends in the next pasture? And does the outcome of that sagging fence mean delivering lambs in the dead of winter, then hunting for newborn lambs in an icy pasture?

The Daughter can only hope that digging a little deeper for an answer that's not obvious will come naturally to her children. And such signs are already evident when the children reject her suggestion to take as a matter of faith the given that a negative times a negative is a positive.

 George

The Daughter leans on her push broom to sweep the bird remains into a corner of the barn then stops to listen in case The Mother's car is crunching its way up the long gravel driveway. Along with bits of dust, hay and fur, she collects the remains into an oversized shovel and dumps it into the trash bucket. Finally, she tips over a hay bale and sits down near the door. She wonders how she could be so tired before 9 AM. Five more minutes she tells herself and then she'll shovel the horse paddock.

Her mind wanders to her children whom she counts on to mature into compassionate human beings. After confronting all the thorny ethical, legal, and moral issues on the farm, she expects them to line up their ducks in a row about what is kindness, what is natural, and when is it time for sad acceptance. They'll soon arrive at clarity regarding whether to shoot a threatening coyote or an aggressive batch of hammering woodpeckers intent on tearing apart the house. They'll know the manmade laws as well and will determine the best way to handle hawks that threaten to dive bomb and steal Theresa, the daredevil chicken who lays those precious blue eggs. They'll gather the courage to call the veterinarian to put down a favorite horse that has gone blind from  Lyme and can no longer navigate in the snow and ice with electric fences and slippery hills. They'll know without a question what's best for the animal and defer, however sadly, to that answer.

Decisions like these will force her children to sacrifice comfortable feelings and trade them for adult sorrows. They'll be too numerous to count but along the way to adulthood, they will have learned that doing the right thing is hard. But on the plus side, each lesson will translate into an answer for the adult world. What The Daughter has learned the hard way, they'll already know. At least, this is The Daughter's plan.

Doubt does creep in during times of exhaustion when The Daughter wonders if all this knowledge is somehow an unwelcome gift? Should she be subjecting her children to a succession of frightful lessons instead of protecting them from bloody births, deaths of pets, and burials in the lonely ground of winter? But then she recovers her will as she sees her children already changing for the better. They no longer procrastinate. Animals need food and water even if it's raining and the children would rather be watching television than shoveling a scoop of food for a whining dog. Predators don't wait for morning to hunt if a fence goes down in the night.

She teaches her children by example but has to approach The Mother in more deliberate ways, often metaphorical. It means a lot to The Daughter for her mother to understand, and she continues to explain in ways that may reposition her mother toward conscious reasoning and understanding.

Farming's like mountain climbing, The Daughter tells her mother. The climber thinks more than one step ahead so as not to fall over a precipice. Then, she trades the metaphor for the game of bridge that her mother knows well. A farmer also must think smart and more than one step ahead to stay out of trouble. The Mother guesses her partner's strong suit based on opening bids, but then she may be forced to sacrifice a trump now in order to win the game.

Risk is a fact of life since everything may go haywire in spite of careful planning. In the case of the farmer, the gods of nature are in charge just as they are with her patchy spinal column and brain. Like the hidden saxifrage splitting an otherwise solid rock, plans can be undermined by an unanticipated hailstorm, selenium deficit, or the arrival of triplets instead of twins. Nature is arbitrary and that's why those holes and pits need to be dug before the ground freezes over.

Scratching the Surface

The Mother's phone rings at 7 AM. The Daughter has been awake and in the barn for two hours but out of respect has waited to call her mother. She reports that a bolt of lightning has fried her electric fence and she'll be working in the barn to rebuild the charger. The Mother wonders if she's calling for sympathy.

"Maybe you should reconsider your line of work," was The Mother's comment. As usual, the daughter let it roll over and off. Instead, "As long as you're awake, come on over and pick up some eggs. The girls are going crazy."

ः

While crossing the ravine through the woods and snaking up the driveway into the roundabout in front of the house, The Mother sees the approach as a museum painting that lends itself toward impressionistic pastels in the spring and Hudson River School with the golds and oranges of autumn. Then she changes her mind and decides the view is more like a work of conceptual art, a Japanese garden with evenly raked rows and manicured specimen trees.

The bucolic farm scene in front of her hadn't just appeared but was created purposefully by The Daughter. The enormity of the effort, the sacrifice of time and the required energy troubles The Mother. To her, the Farm is of marginal benefit.

The Mother hears her heartbeat as she steps out of the car and into the stillness. She remains silent for a moment before closing her car door. Out of respect, for what or for whom?

Mouse remains are nowhere to be seen. The chickens are scratching in the dirt and hopping backwards every few seconds to get an exact fix on a fresh grub supply from underneath an over-turned bucket. Sheep graze on fresh pasture, and Theresa, the in-dependent chicken who has learned how to leap the electric fence, pecks her way around the base of the house in a game of hide and seek as she locates a secret place to lay her precious blue egg.

The horses' noses are stuck in the grass. The coon cats are nowhere in sight. The tomatoes silently spread up and outside their cages while a neighboring row of wax beans wind their tendrils up strings at least a foot a day. The weeding stool has fallen onto its side in the middle of the garden rows as if abandoned quickly for a phone call, a clap of thunder or a threatening horsefly. Empty rock-ing chairs on the porch move in unison in the gentle morning breeze scented with the familiar fragrance of fresh hay. For the moment The Mother's world and that of The Daughter is in harmony.

The scent of lilac entices The Mother toward the bouquet of bushes behind the kitchen. Could she ever become accustomed to this deafening quiet, the kind of stillness where one becomes an interloper and in which thoughts are louder than the humming of insects? And since many, maybe the majority, of her thoughts are worries, what-ifs, and then-whats, isn't she better off distracted by city sounds, phone calls, and blasts of television news alerts?

She is so unlike her daughter who prefers being alone with herself and stuck, by her own choice, out in the country without a pharmacy or supermarket within ten miles?

The Mother reminds herself that she's come to pick up fresh eggs.

ʚɞ

Spring in Upstate New York is short. The Mother has a vision of the summer crop of vegetables like those prickly cucumbers that drove The Daughter mad last year with their abundance. Then the zucchini of all sizes arrived, some as big around as baseball bats.

She gathered bowls of tiny round orange or pear shaped yellow tomatoes, bunches of giant sunflowers, and too many green and yellow beans. But those sugar snap peas, The Mother believes, have always won the blue ribbon prize. She had a fleeting thought to grow a personal row of them next year.

The Mother walks through the kitchen and past an ice bucket full of syringes too close to the breadboard, she thinks. They're loaded with protective serum for the new babies due this day. And next to them rests a baby bottle of thick yellow colostrum for Joan Rivers' lambs that will need a better start than their sick, though very loud and clever, mother will be able to provide.

The black Labrador retriever, loveable guide dog reject, who allowed his trainer to walk in front of a bus during his final test, opens one eye as The Mother heads outside to the barn. His young friend, a yellow lab, another guide dog reject who failed the hotdog avoidance test, is equally bored and is curled up under the desk waiting for someone's feet to sit on.

The Mother is rehearsing and determined to tell her daughter that she works too hard. She will say exactly that. Usually she rolls out a platitude like, "you're overdoing it" or "what's the rush...your work will wait," or, "please sit for a minute and keep me company." Today she'll be firm and tell her daughter she must give her body a rest.

The Daughter is still in the barn with the electric charger in pieces on a tray atop a hay bale. She's working her Phillips screw driver to replace the cover. She's not in her kitchen rustling up a garden to table breakfast for the family.

"What have I done with those fly masks?" The Daughter scans the barn walls and sees them hanging just where they belong. The mother recoils and waves her hand around her own face as if to ward off an attack.

"It's just that time of year," The Daughter tells her mother who grew up with Oriental rugs and out of habit picks her way around the barn floor to avoid clumps of God knows what.

"Soon it will be the deer flies," The Mother says as she recalls the bloodthirsty squadron last year that chased her down the driveway to the mailbox on the golf cart. Those things should be the subject of a slasher horror movie for the terror they pose.

As The Daughter velcros the masks onto each horse, their ears already bloodied by bites from the newly hatched black flies, she describes the wild turkey hens who are gobbling her grass seed as fast as they're able. "It's a losing cause, I'm afraid, unless Buckwheat decides to have extra people around his Thanksgiving table."

The Daughter is referring to the neighbor on her favorites list who enjoys wild turkey dinners and in his spare time takes apart and recalibrates malfunctioning farm equipment. He doesn't write legal briefs but can fix the weld on a broken piece in the pump and make it hum in the dead of winter. Buckwheat's the kind of neighbor who will notice if there are no tire tracks in the fresh snow and will check to see if your car's stuck or has slid into the ravine.

Already this morning, storm clouds are blowing in from the west. "The rain will finish off any remaining seeds," The Daughter tells her mother who doesn't respond because anything and everything she could or would say has been said. It's always a variation of "What possesses you to work this farm? Any farm for that matter?" The Daughter then walls herself into defense mode and the conversations never make forward progress.

"Did you notice that I smashed an egg all over the chicken food?" The Daughter continues. "These girls will just have to survive because I have to get ahead of the storm."

She glances out the stall door to see dark clouds forming in the distance. Even The Mother has learned that the sheep must be in the barn and dry when Fred comes to shear. But getting them in and sorted, the right mamas with the right babies, is no easy chore.

The Daughter scans the wall of the barn next to the empty nail where her fly masks had been, but the shepherd's crook is not where it belongs. The Mother sees it propped up against some hay bales, reaches it easily, and hands it off to her daughter in order to save her a few steps.

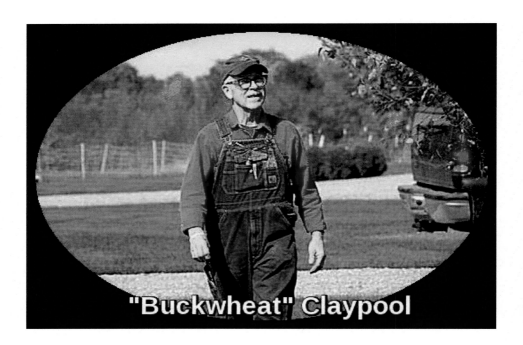

"Buckwheat" Claypool

You Can Lead A Horse To Water And Make Her Thirsty

As she comes by the farm more often, The Mother confesses to an occasional twinge of enlightenment. That small spark of understanding, unwelcome as it is, alarms her. She'll never agree with the hard work and disappointments of a farmer. How could she ever accept that it's worthwhile to cater to an animal, pamper it and still watch it die in spite of all the colostrum, wormings, minerals, kelp, and attention to detail? How could she imagine that harmless hay can kill with its lurking listeria? "Frankly," she tells her daughter, "worrying about hay is one of those unnecessary activities. You're creating your own hell. Don't you have a million other things that would be more fun to worry about than hay?"

Unspoken by The Mother is a continuous thread of her own of fears for her daughter. Will it rain before Farmer Smith hays her fields? Is he going to get to the second cut? How much hay will she need? Who is going to help her unload and stack the hay? Shouldn't she core her hay for analysis?

"You must have hay dreams," The Mother laughs at the thought and then not jokingly says, "Stress is known to wreak havoc on the body and you're putting yourself under enormous stress. If you would just teach school, you could worry about lesson plans that you're able to control."

"I'm more than qualified to deal with hay issues." The sharp tongue of The Daughter's teenage years adds, "Save your anxiety for worrying about where to go for lunch." She believes that her mother who sees herself as highly evolved is really in the process of spinning out and away from a life that matters.

Barn swallows flutter in and out of the barn that The Daughter designed to her exact specifications. For a moment The Mother gives it up, takes a breath of barn air, and chooses to remember those twittering swallows of her childhood as they flew in formation attached to the hem of Cinderella's ball gown.

The Daughter follows her mother's gaze upward to the busy swallows in the rafters. Then she looks toward the post where she's set an empty barn swallow nest loomed in entirety by one tiny beak. The fine piece of nonhuman weaving is lined with tiny feathers, puffs of down, and bits of silky wool snatched from the backs of her lambs. She is forced to appreciate the brazen little thieves sneaking black and brown horsehairs to bind the nest into a natural craft form that rivals that of the finest weavers.

The Daughter lifts the nest down to show The Mother its intricate interior as she points her camera to capture its beauty in the best light.

Making Hay While the Sun Shines

The Daughter remains focused on her mission in spite of The Mother's not-so-silent disapproval. She delights in the fulfillment of her vision that includes passing along her values to her children while indulging her own needs for connection with the land in the here and now. The Mother tells her she must have sabra genetics and knows she would have been the perfect candidate to lay drainage tiles in Palestine alongside her great great grandfather. The Daughter would have indeed taken pleasure in laying out the orange groves. She would have dowsed the deepest new wells and might have trained the camels to stop spitting.

Those concentric wave circles that originally consigned The Mother to the perimeter looking toward The Daughter at the center are flattening over time with tempered dialogue, fewer judgments, more empathy and a shared delight in the images captured on The Mother's camera. Always fearing the center stone that is her daughter will sink and drown under the weight of the farm and chores, The Mother is surprised lately by her own ability to minimize the number of her directives as well as a newfound willingness to drop former complaints.

While the Daughter continues to wrestle with her physical surroundings, both she and her mother photograph the ever-changing tangibles that populate the farm world as if to be certain to capture it all before it vanishes and fades into the next season. From all angles and in all light they photograph the stacks of wax beans and green beans on the kitchen counter. They note the beauty in the soldier like order of Mason jars waiting to be stuffed with a new crop of dilly beans. They strategize together the best way to capture in the dramatic light the fledgling birds whose nests are found in the strangest of locations. And they regard their poopkin photos as heavenly metaphors. What else sprouts from last year's composting pumpkin mash that defines so clearly the presence of a kindly, perhaps orange, God? The renewable surprise each year deserves a documenting photo.

The Daughter cannot always grab her camera in the rush of the touch and go lambing season. The blessed events, the birthing of colorful babies of black, white, mouflon, moorit, and combinations thereof, emerge after she has prepared all winter. And with the lambs born and nurtured, the time comes to mine the seed catalogues for new varieties of vegetables to plant in the garden. The Daughter suspects that particular process is akin to The Mother in her heyday spending the day playing through new piano editions at the music store.

α

By summertime The Mother is nudged and teased by the colors in the garden…and the smell of freshly cut hay and lanolin from

the wool…and the ribald stories from the charming sheep shearer, Vermont Fred. The Mother slows down for a few minutes now and then to recognize her own limited worldview and owns a tinge of nagging shame that it's taking her so long to come to acceptance. She is, after all, The Mother who raised this child of hers and as such has agreed to take full responsibility for the Daughter's decision to gather her specific variety of rosebuds.

α

The Mother is fascinated as the flock of sheep race toward The Daughter-Whisperer who rattles the grain bucket and sings out, "Here Sheepies." Their devotion to their shepherdess who brings them food and scratches their backs suggests a subliminal conversation and reciprocity that is touching. But The Mother continues to worry as it becomes more complicated for The Daughter to work the farm especially in the heat of the summers. It's not exactly a simple pleasure to harvest a bumper vegetable crop when The Daughter has to create and manage it herself with only weekend help from the husband and children, now teenagers. And, thank God for Buckwheat, the village savior, as close to a saint as Jude when all seems lost. He quietly floats above and around the hubbub, an angel in overalls in a red pickup truck, assessing the damage, and firing up his welding torch when necessary.

The farm chores are never ending, but The Daughter insists the cycle has its rewards. She remembers to backhoe out those empty graves before the freeze sets in to prepare for unanticipated loss; she drains the hoses for winter and double checks the condition of her heaters for the water buckets. She has organized her calendar to be ready again for the first lamb deliveries. Her list is long and she is walking slowly using her stick for balance.

cg

The Daughter comforts her skeptical mother that a good farmer is as smart in many ways as her Ivy League college classmates who clerk for a justice, plan political strategies, or write grants to continue funding their basic research. Timing, planning and organizing is key, as well, to managing a sustainable farm. And what's more, The Daughter knows, and The Mother is learning, that it's just the luck of the draw if a water well, carefully witched and sited with a forked stick, flows with water or with methane. She also knows it's a crapshoot that determines whether or not her myelin will stick around to carry uninterrupted messages from one part of her body to another.

The notion of chance is difficult for The Mother to accept for she believes she's been successful in the past in controlling some of the world around her. The truth, of course, is far different: The Mother has merely harvested more than her fair share of good luck.

The Mother sees tedium in changing pasture fencing every week or gathering eggs every day and detailing the coop now and then. The Daughter recoils at the thought of braving mobs of people at concerts, parades, and airports. Instead, watching her healthy flock of ewes, lambs and rams dining on fresh grass and knowing that she's had a small hand in it triggers a feeling in The Daughter she can't even describe to The Mother whose head spins with overloaded city circuits. She sees only drudgery in her daughter's world.

The Daughter is curious and asks her mother one evening at dusk, "Do you see this light?" She looks out from the back pens to the sheep grazing beside the barn over toward the chickens and vegetable gardens. The ten acres fields behind the house are a patchwork defined by old stone walls in varying states of disrepair. "Look how the light bounces with the breeze. I can't decide if I love the early morning light better. Which do you like better?" This evening's early light seemed to glow gold.

The Mother is silent while watching her daughter.

"Mother, please. Don't look at me...look at the light. Don't you see the light?"

The Mother replies, "Of course I can see the light. You know that."

The Daughter says, "Be still, then and soon you'll hear it, too." She knows it may take more patience to wait, to listen and to hear.

For the Daughter the transformation from dark to light, from old pasture to fresh pasture, rain to sunshine and rainbows, snow to mud, mud to sprouts; from snow covered fields to lush green and from her barn overloaded with hay to one with a diminishing inventory, flake by flake...this ebb and flow defines her satisfaction. There's always something coming into bloom or something being born or the ending of a life cycle.

The photo at the end of any spring, summer, or autumn day captures an exhausted farmer relaxing in the rocking chair next to her husband on the front porch. In her lap is nestled Theresa. She smells fresh hay and sees a bright Venus sprout in the heavens at the horizon.

Bee In Her Bonnet

The Mother understood aspirations. She dared to have them and that's why she hung her framed diploma from her Ivory Tower women's college over the toilet. It was hardly a joyful statement but more an indicator of her belief she was the victim of a conspiracy of her generation to keep her in her harvest gold kitchen or 20 feet away in her piano studio. One ee and a, two ee and a. Tapity tapity tapity tah-ah. She spent hours in that small place within the large world she'd only read about, but where balance and counting out loud with hands separate before hands together were basic values based on a belief system that discipline alongside hard work was king. It was the place where memorization wasn't a haphazard occurrence after a student played a piece of music ad nauseam but where the composition was deliberately deconstructed, analyzed, and then reassembled with the correct portatos and rubatos. In that studio, time and again, she reminded her students not to overdo the emotion in Chopin or pound Strauss like an oompah band. Finesse was hard to teach.

Music is usually predictable and annotated for musicians and teachers like her to interpret as best they can. The Mother appreciates the directives spelled out by the composers, all of which lead her forward in an orderly way. By ironing out rough spots, transitions and unclear dynamics, The Mother extinguishes her anxiety not just in her music but in her life. Dissonance gets resolved through practice and rehearsals.

Her music is a nearly perfect counterpoint to The Daughter's farm, for there, at any moment and without notice, chaos is apt to break out. But her daughter prefers the unpredictability of nature. Learning to cope, she says, is how she

gets in touch with what is human inside her and adds to her satisfying store of knowledge.

Except in the safety of her studio or kitchen, there were few other places The Mother could speak of her aspirations that were really intangible longings running alongside a thin ribbon of hope. The longings, she feared, would never be realized and the hope was for a talent to surface now and then. It would come in the form of an enthusiastic student worthy of her time and energy and would provide a rational alternative to the kitchen. If it were ever to arrive, it would float in, a deus ex machina, and bring along the satisfaction that she had inspired a truly emotional response to the beautiful music being studied.

In those days, most men and women believed that The Mother was exactly where she belonged, waiting at home for a call from the school that her child had vomited or had chewed her ring into a pretzel shape or was tossing his lunch into the trashcan every day.

The Mother recalls with a strange combination of pride and irritation how a pediatrician neighbor would come by to collect his child from a play date and hang out in her kitchen eating her warm chocolate chip cookies. He was grateful to accept a glass of cold milk to wash them down. "I wish my wife would stay home with the kids and bake cookies," he'd said.

At that point, it would have been unkind for The Mother to reveal that his wife was the focus of nasty gossip as she left home everyday for graduate school in pursuit of a PhD. Such aspirations were not highly regarded by the ladies of the neighborhood.

ଓ

When The Daughter was born, The Mother raised her with great care according to the agenda of the times. As a fan of Stone and Church in Child Study 101, she thanked God for the parenting experts, Spock, Ginott, and Dobson. She delighted in the antics of her baby daughter. Even when the toddler was at the stage of throwing her empty silver cup halfway across the kitchen while yelling, "All gone," The Mother only laughed while saying no-no. She silently admired her baby's strong throwing arm.

The Mother insisted on old-fashioned standards of honesty although there were several breeches by The Daughter during her teenage years when she ended up at a field party rather the library or a rock concert in another city rather than her girlfriend's house. She'd be suspended from the car or given hard labor of washing windows or pulling weeds, but The Mother held her ground and stressed the importance of maintaining high ethical standards, respect for the elderly, her teachers, and animals even though she herself was highly allergic to cats and afraid of big dogs. Thank you notes were written promptly with a minimum of pressure even after overhearing The Daughter refer to her on the phone with her friends as The Gestapo.

While The Daughter's bedroom walls were draped in black fabric, possibly a rebellious f--- you to The Mother and other adults who preferred pastels, the walls underneath remained pristine. The Daughter cleaned her room and laundered her waterbed sheets on Sundays as per unwritten contract. Always vigilant, The Mother averted house fires by unburying a hot curling iron from underneath towels after the careless daughter rushed off to school. Fines, or groundings from the curling iron, or labeling her an unmitigated slob did little to limit the teenaged daughter's free spirit.

Otherwise, The Daughter was exemplary in every way except that she was spending all her free time at the stables mucking her stall, picking hooves, braiding a mane, or galloping around the fields with her horse buddies. She balked at demands to practice the piano until she quit lessons entirely in spite of her unusual talent. Her memory could easily corral thirty pages of a piano concerto and her ability to perform under pressure signaled to the Mother a promising career in piano performance. The Daughter would toss back her hair and run her strong fingers up and down the keyboard with ferocious velocity and accurate dynamics. But, still she lacked the honest passion of a dedicated musician.

Barking Up The Wrong Tree

While The Daughter had been bribed with colorful nail polish as a young child and restricted from the horse until she did her time at the piano, no one could intervene to keep the now 14-year-old daughter committed to her music. The jig was up and the piano lid was closed for good. While The Daughter felt relief, The Mother wept as if her child was Pavarotti dedicating himself to soccer over opera. She wondered why anyone with such talent didn't recognize an obligation to share it with the world.

In hindsight the Mother realizes she'd ignored obvious warnings over the years, small red flags signaling that The Daughter would be winning every future battle. The piece of lettuce stuck to a salad bowl should have trumpeted what was to come. That time the six year old had been sent to her room until she agreed to taste the piece of lettuce. The Daughter at that young age prevailed by clamping her mouth shut. The lettuce finally glued itself to the bottom of the bowl until The Mother removed it days later in quiet defeat. Any semblance of control and future planning that The Mother had assumed was in her job description was rinsed down the kitchen drain alongside the desiccated piece of lettuce.

Having learned at her Ivory Tower college that nurturing a child correctly could override all natural tendencies, The Mother never really gave up her attempts to shape her Daughter as well as the world around them. And who could blame the Mother for trying to turn that world into a more hospitable place

for both of them. Despite anecdotal evidence to the contrary, academics of the day believed that Nurture ruled the roost over Nature, but The Mother, like every loving parent, wanted to believe that anything and everything was possible for her child and that, like it or not, it included becoming a farmer.

A Silk Purse Out of A Sow's Ear

The Daughter has become a real farmer with a barn, neatly stacked hay, two barn kitties, Icelandic horses who are trained to tolt, chickens, a lot of sheep, golf carts for hauling heavy buckets to compost, a poop pile that magically produces gorgeous pumpkins (or poopkins as The Daughter calls them), a zero turn tractor, a spinning wheel and freezers filled with five star lamb from her grass fed flock.

Picture book views stretch across the patchwork of her ten-acre fields defined by crumbling colonial stone walls. A beaver dam, a ravine, and a stand of old birch trees show no evidence of the existence of the old still. The bare bones of a coyote and the gnarled apple orchard, now at least a century old, are useless remnants on the farm and exist now only to spook the children on Halloween. Whether covered with snow, hay bales, or lawn, the fields are Grandma Moses photo ops, not flatly primitive, but maybe just too nearly perfect.

The Daughter, and now The Mother, have been toting their cameras everywhere they go on the farm. They wait for early or late light, ethereal shadows and color, an unexpected rainbow or a stiff wind. They spot deer and parades of turkey families while hawks and owls threaten Theresa and her chicken friends. Odd tracks and scat provide an unending supply of mysteries. The Daughter and The Mother are stealthy lookers who see the same things through their respective lenses. They're connected as never before to the land and to each other with their shared goal of the fixing sacred moments in their unique ways. A pumpkin on the manure pile from last year's garbage, a child measuring herself against a giant sunflower, two toes and a nose in a perfect lambing are all welcomed subjects. A mother and her daughter, head to head, compare photo images.

During autumn haying The Mother and The Daughter worry in unison for the safety of the fawn who lies abandoned in the center of a field while loud machinery works around her. Will the doe retrieve her at dusk or will it be a Bambi style ending with a coyote dashing into the field? The Mother still prefers a gentle predictability while The Daughter is willing to watch the scenario play out as nature chooses.

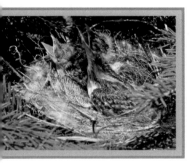

In the springtime The Daughter rolls by her Japanese maples on her golf cart and hears a distinct tweeting. She notices tiny beaks open straight up in the new nest and at the same moment out of the corner of her eye she notices her rambunctious ram has leaped the electric fence that appears yet again to have shorted out. "Yet again" and "yet again." How often she's aware of the ironic juxtaposition of the sacred and the profane, the blessing and the curse. On the farm, it's not complicated to tease out the precious from the worthless.

It's just too bad she's no longer nimble enough to capture photos from atop her stepladder of these fledglings or, even more exciting, her ram's high jump midway up and over the electric fence to surprise his girlfriends in the next field.

ଓଃ

Musings are important but at this moment The Daughter has no choice but to rebuild her doomed and godforsaken charging box and to do it as quickly as possible. Then she'll get to her golf cart, grab her shepherd's crook and corral the ram back into his personal space while someone, maybe her mother in a team effort, will head him off from the other direction. She walks slowly and drags one leg that is unable to follow her orders to bend at the knee. She hopes she'll have time for today's weekly feces inspection in the kitchen before the children come home for cookies and milk. According to the experts at last year's spring parasite conference, it's way past time.

She's learned a lot in spite of the teasing she endured from her family as the conference entry fee had been a Mother's Day gift from her mother, the piano teacher. Unlike the gift certificate that her friends received for an algae wrap at the spa, this parasite conference was perfect for her with its informative lists of local farming resources. The Daughter loved the topic and took pride in being the only participant in attendance that day without a beard and suspenders.

Within the hour The Daughter has tired and moves at half speed to set up the microscope. She rests for a long moment before she summons the courage to force herself onto her feet.

αβ

The Daughter no longer considers The Mother's vision of success costumed in a judge's robe or a professor's lab coat. That's been composted along with the dead sheep or buried in a cloud pile of long fibered fleece ready to send to the mill. Lear jets and peer-reviewed articles in JAMA are now far from her mind and that of her mother. The children accept the natural order of life and death. Her reject guide dog that ate eight corncobs has died of cancer and not an intestinal blockage.

The kids cry and bury their animals. Then they move on. They see how their mother enjoys caring for the animals, a pleasure tempered, but not extinguished, when she loses a fine animal to sickness or old age. Compassion, patience, diligence, attention to detail. They're learning what their mother, the farmer, calls the shovel ethic.

Counting Her Chickens

The Mother steps carefully around the dog crate in the back hall. One of the "girls," Theresa, is confined within and clucks her heart out while echoes reverberate throughout the house. The Daughter murmurs, "I think an egg's coming on." Sure enough, the egg is laid but without its shell. Something is obviously wrong with this chicken, skinny as a garden stake and bespeckled with blood where feathers were supposed to be attached. With that affliction, she's as vulnerable among her former friends as an outed undercover agent, for seeing red sends them into a murderous rage. This girl is now under house arrest for her own good.

The Daughter's husband, his head in his hands, tries to concentrate on his computer monitor as he works in his home office next door to the back hall where the former free range, and now outraged ingrate, Theresa, is bellyaching. In the living room the son's yellow and green parakeets, an alternative gift to the X-Box from Santa, are trying to outscream Theresa. But their chatterings are a far cry from Theresa's overarching racket. This audio pecking order keeps the husband at the bottom of the heap while The Daughter laughs at the Darwinian notion of survival of the fittest or the alternate notion of who is best able to adapt within the given environment. There's no question about who is the loser.

And while Theresa has once known the view from the top of the ladder, a fit Rhode Island Red among a clutch that allowed equal opportunity for all to challenge her, a new order has emerged. With Theresa's laying days ending due to chicken menopause, Theresa's unsympathetic girlfriends are blind to the fact that their day will be coming soon enough. Had they not all arrived together at the post office? All the same size and stuffed into the same shallow box? Hadn't they all been equal partners in the dark? Only Theresa knows that she may have the last laugh.

What has formerly been a charmed life for a princess of a chicken who dined on buckets of organic garden throwaways is now but a memory for the proud Theresa. When she'd arrived, her new home was the recently assembled coop on wheels, another Mother's Day bonanza for The Daughter. It joined The Daughter's crook, a giant fan for the horses, and enough hay in the barn until the next harvest.

Now Theresa needs protection from her nasty former girl-friends who smell the rat of weakness. No longer able to wander freely, she's left screaming mad and humiliated in a used dog crate. The Daughter knows that if she were a real farmer, this sick chick, Theresa, now with an uncertain future, would have been in a stock-pot long before her relationship troubles began.

The Daughter is annoyed with herself for her lack of fore-sight. There are no extra small holes prepared in the frozen ground since the soup pot was unimaginable for this loyal and hard working Rhode Island Red.

The seasons change yet everything and nothing stays the same.

No Eggs in the Basket

W hite pelicans have descended into the cove outside The Mother's Florida lanai, their private rookery but a stone's throw. In competition with the local fish house with its nets and flat bottom boat, the huge birds nosedive for the plentiful mullet while risking a broken neck in their daredevil swoop, grab, and swallow routine. Although The Mother is comfortable in a warm winter climate, when she looks out her own windows 1,351 miles away from her daughter, she feels too far away, especially during this frigid and snowy winter. She's unconnected and disconnected from the farm. She's anxious.

Today's phone call from The Daughter engages her mother as a participant rather than a bystander watching a familiar scene like one from an old book of nursery rhymes. They laugh together as The Daughter describes the plight of naïve teenagers who are starting up a goat farm around the corner. When their new goat babies were coated with mud, the excited new farmers decided to shampoo those babies and towel them dry, thereby completely disguising the smell of the babies from the disappointed mama goat who wondered why her new babies disappeared. All those maternal goat hormones producing milk and no babies to nurture made for a sad scene.

The Daughter and her mother shared their common vision of the teenagers bottle feeding those baby goats and blaming each other in the middle of the night for the clever idea to shampoo the muddy babies. They share a laugh together about the debacle and wish they'd had their cameras to capture the scene. In truth, The Daughter admits to her own fiascoes as a novice.

ോ

While it's not quite spring in the North Country, The Daughter calculates out loud. If she were to order her new chicks this morning, they'll arrive in a few days and will be laying by mid-August. The Mother hears excitement in her voice, reminiscent of her daughter as a child who revived all half dead or neglected animals and insects.

It feels just right to The Mother, still too far away, to be invited into her daughter's decision-making process. It comforts her to a large degree to act as a sounding board although she's not the least bit qualified to render a decision never mind a suggestion.

"My old girls won't be laying many more eggs, so, if I get this maternity ward set up in the laundry room, plug in the heat lamps, we'll…" The Daughter interrupts herself. "Gotta go…a sheep's down." She instinctively has been scanning her fields while on the phone. The windows of her farmhouse provide views in all directions and offer visual insurance against predators, escapee sheep or anything out of the ordinary like a hawk circling the wayward Theresa who hops the electric fence to expand her personal worldview.

"Bring your cell phone," The Mother raises her voice reflexively as her daughter drops the receiver to rush into a brutal early spring cold snap. Knowing it's windy with a temperature in the single digits, The Mother's words trail to a whisper but the call has ended. She'd been too late to say, "Call me the minute you get indoors."

A half hour passes and The Mother tries to block out ugly scenarios of a slip on the icy hill or a broken bone with no one due home until 5 PM. The Mother fights her dark side and dreads becoming the caricature of the prophet of doom. Still, she's unable to scrub from her obsessive memory the nightmare story she'd heard decades earlier. That scenario sets up with an avid young duck hunter, the brother of her friend, outfitted from Orvis in his plaid jacket and warm hat, 12-gauge shotgun on his shoulder and duck whistles clipped to the chest pocket of his vest. He waits patiently in his waist high waders, the sun in the swamps of Louisiana bright in mid-afternoon. But by the next morning he has frozen and when finally discovered, he's lifeless and standing upright like a Madame Tussauds mannequin. The Mother tries to shake off the horror of the visual.

If her daughter possessed a normal spinal column instead of one spattered with senseless interruptions, The Mother might worry less. Or would she? In truth, hyper-vigilance is likely embedded in the fabric of her DNA along with her personal brand of memory that doesn't store neutral information such as the digits for pi or the calendar for the new year. Instead, her particular atavistic memory hoards useless information such as details of Old Country pogroms, people choking to death on popcorn, or worse.

When The Mother's phone rings, The Daughter says simply, "I'm in. I'll call later." Her voice is tearful and that explains everything to this mother who can read her daughter's every look or the tone of her voice. A sheep has died and the unborn triplet lambs in her womb, only a month before delivery, have died with her. The suffering of The Daughter at times like this is conveyed to her mother as though they were in fact conjoined.

While The Daughter has always claimed a complete acceptance of the natural cycle of life, the dangers of the elements as well as oddball pregnancies that don't end well, she grieves the loss of every animal. As the midwife, she helps bring each baby into the world with her towels, hairdryer, and her packaged colostrum. She roughs up the little ones till they bleat and bounce to their feet. But today in the icy pasture in a trench beside three feet of snow with no hope of survival for her unborn triplets, this mouflon sheep is lifeless.

Through her tears, The Daughter musters her pragmatist farmer self. The hole has been dug but she can't find it under the snow pack and who, she wonders, will do the tractor work with her husband out of town? Even in the cold, this favored animal will attract coyotes to the fields. Will she need the rifle to fend off scavengers? Will she need to call Buckwheat to come in his pickup truck to help her drag the sheep to the barn or lift it into his truck or into the trunk of her car?

The Daughter's pain once again has been distributed to The Mother later in the day as she hears of the bloated sheep lying on her side in the snow-covered pasture. Loss, grief, frustration, blame. All of the emotions exhaust The Mother when there is no possibility of convincing her daughter to let go of this life, the life that so many people claim is exactly their dream job, especially in retirement. How quaint, they think, to gather colorful eggs every day. How splendid to view horses in one photo op after another, neck to neck, munching on fresh grass or frolicking in a thunderous gallop. How calming, they believe, to listen to the bah-bah sheepies who bounce toward the barn to the tune of a shaken pan of feed.

Little do they know what The Mother knows about digging holes in the fall for animals that die during harsh winters. Or, what do they know about gates wedged shut by deep snow and ice, or about coyotes that come too close if they get a whiff of a fresh placenta lying in the field. Transformers blow up and loveable kitties disappear. And in the ironic circle of food-chain politics, baby birds are hunted and devoured by those cute Maine Coon polydactyl kitties.

The Mother realizes that she's the one who had better work harder on letting go. It is she, with her all-encompassing love for her grown child, who is doomed to an added layer of suffering. The top layer, a visitor view, is nothing but a relatively easy Buddhist style acceptance of the fact that parents don't get to pick the children they get. While some get economists or lawyers, others get farmers and with them the cycle of life and death and suffering. That cycle, no matter how natural, threatens to overwhelm both The Mother and The Daughter.

The Mother is not yet convinced that the bounty of fresh vegetables, clean eggs, antibiotic and hormone free meat, spring blooms, and the witness to the triumphant engineering of the birds' nests trump the miseries of The Farmer.

Beauty Is In The Eye of the Beholder

Years ago The Mother had arrived at the farm as a guest and was sometimes seen as a hostile interloper. She'd leave with her beans, eggs, hydrangea, or lamb roasts. As the seasons changed and the years went by, The Mother gradually warmed to the natural wonders on her daughter's property, first through the lens of her camera and then without the help of the camera. Now The Mother adds photos of stonewalls, autumn sumac, and fledgling robins to her normal takeaways of vegetables, eggs and meat. She glories in the fresh breezes from a rocking chair on the porch (the smells are what they are) and her latest photos are of animals. She laughs happily as she watches the children helping with the chickens, the garden harvest, and the birthing of a lamb when a ewe needs help.

The Mother has learned not to panic when she hears a howling coyote, and like her daughter, she goes on high alert if a hawk or fox is eyeing a chicken. In good times she stands alongside her grandchildren in the garden twisting off and eating sugar snap peas without washing them. She's pleased to be able to speak with authority about the weather and how it has influenced the garden…or the haying and the second cut…or the animals and the ram whose babies all have inherited sharp teeth.

She can also tell how wet or dry the summer if the corn is knee high by the 4th of July. She knows the minute spring arrives because she hears the chirping of peepers from the many ponds in the surrounding farmland. She has no need for news from a groundhog in Punxsutawney, Pennsylvania.

The Mother listens and learns. One day she remarks

that even though the wax beans are stunted and the beetles are ruining the kale and gourd seeds have infiltrated the summer squash seeds, at least the morning glories are spectacular. And then she nearly crows, "Your new ram has given us incredible lambs."

ᨣ

The Mother remembers how her daughter pulled on a pair of long gloves to deliver her now dead ewe's firstborn, turning her from breech position and tugging her onto the hay covered floor of the stall. She toweled off that lamb and put the lazy lamb to her mother to nurse immediately. It is that cycle of life and death, spring to winter, summer to fall that means so much to her daughter, The Farmer, who continues to teach her mother, now a willing learner, why Halloween colors are yellows and purples and why one must never shampoo a dirty baby goat or sheep. The Mother has learned the difference between a Phillips screwdriver and a regular screwdriver but recently gave up on her attempt to fix the fence charger when she discovered a leftover screw. "Let's throw this damn thing out and order a new one!"

The Daughter sees progress and holds no grudge since there is no mother anywhere who knows what she's going to birth. A black or spotted lamb? A polydactyl Hemingway barn kitty? Or a daughter who's a farmer teaching her mother compassion for the land and how to enjoy the privilege of taking part in the process of life and production.

Every day The Farmer welcomes a different set of challenges, for she believes change prevents her life from becoming routine. Tapity tah-ah. She never takes for granted a harvest moon on a warm summer night, and she has faith that her children will never take it for granted either.

Epilogue:

The Mother recently attended her Ivory Tower college reunion and when asked about her daughter, she told her old friends without apology, "My daughter's a farmer," and she left it at that. She didn't mention that she herself sweeps up remains in the barn, has mastered the skills to deliver an oversized lamb, tie up beans, and repair an electric fence. Neither did she mention that she laughs harder than her daughter when she notices a reversed pecking order. The dog wolfs down the cat's food and drools as he waits respectfully for the cat to finish off his food. And neither did she describe a pleasant and recurring dream of a mother-in-law apartment in the back of The Daughter's house, miles from the nearest supermarket.

The Daughter cannot keep up the fast pace of the farm life. She must rest often, continue to listen to the light and hope that a cure for Multiple Sclerosis is just around the corner.

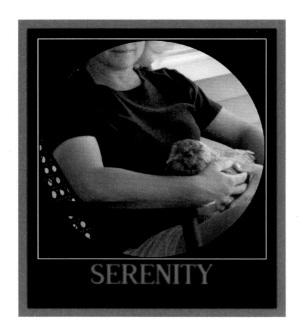

SERENITY

HAPPY HOLIDAYS 2002

We can't believe that it has been over three years since we moved to New York where our life, between children and animals, is quite literally turning into a zoo.

During the past year we've lived out the "nature vs. nurture" debate. Nature wins...hands down. Given our experience with Jen, our expectations around sleep, peace and quiet were rather low when Lil arrived. Thank goodness we were mistaken. From the beginning Lil slept, ate, didn't barf and was pretty much Jen's mirror image. She's approaching the 12-month mark and continues to be the model citizen of our household. Now, on the verge of walking, Lil is a climbing machine. On a daily basis she gets herself stuck in the refrigerator and likes to hang out in the giant basket of dog toys.

Jen continues to evolve into a little person full of energy and enthusiasm and is always on the move. Her big news is that she now "goes to college." She's in the pre-school program of Skidmore College and loves it. When we're getting ready to leave, she climbs into her car seat, bounces up and down, and tells us over and over, "Hurry up! Hurry up! I don't want to miss it!" Lately she's really beginning to use her words along with her priceless expressions. When asked what she thought of Harry, a friend in her class, she replied with a straight face, "He's a pretty cool guy."

And coming this April we're expecting a baby. Other than the species, we don't know or plan to find out what "it" is. Jen has made it quite clear that whiles she's forgiven us for bringing Lil home, she has run out of patience and this time she's expecting a puppy. Luckily, Lil doesn't have a clue as to what's going on.

Instead of a major home improvement project this year, we did a yard project and built a barn. It turned out to be a bit more than we need right now, but we've been warned that horses are a very bad habit and tend to accumulate. We may as well be prepared. In June we added two Icelandic horses (Blakkur and Brandur) to our family. Icelandics are quick, strong, and brave little horses and have yet to find anything they wont go over or through. We've been chased by dogs and cows and have yet to suffer a crisis. They're gaited so in addition to a walk, trot, and canter they also "tolt," an incredibly smooth running walk. Blakkur is dignified and cooperative and Brandur is our litte punk who broke out of his stall to mow the grass two days after he arrived from Iceland in April. Things like apples disgust him, but he'll do anything for a cracker or a slice of bread.

Jake has no news. His status within the pack hierarchy continues to fall, but his attitude remains remarkably cheerful. And yes, he's still a thief- this morning he stole a donut off the kitchen table.

We think that Alan has finally put an end to the saga of the mowing of the grass. He bought a little tractor this fall that should be more than adequate for all our grass cutting, mulch moving, snow plowing, and (shall we politely say) horse related needs. And there is the fun factor of the tractor. It's the reason that $300 battery operated miniatures can be found next to the bikes in Toys R-US. Moving piles of stone dust or poop can almost be fun when there is no shovel or wheelbarrow involved.

I am looking forward to a non-pregnant summer. While at this point I'm probably unable to solve a simple equation, I can recite without hesitation the shoe or diaper size for everyone in the family, as well as their vaccination and/or worming schedules and the amount of formula on hand in the storage room.

We hope this letter finds all of you well and we wish you the best in the coming year!

Love,

Alan, Alyse, Jen, Lil, Jake, Blakkur and Brandur

HAPPY HOLIDAYS 2003

Dear Friends & Family,

As we reflect on the past year, all we can say is WHEW! Our life hurtles between idyllic moments of Americana (complete with a napping dog at our feet) and a street brawl among a heavyweight, featherweight and a paraplegic (Zach can only do the military crawl) all taking place at a zoo.

The highlight of our year came in April when Zach was born. Quite honestly, we wondered what we'd brought into the world because he spent his first few weeks twitchy, red and very, very angry. Thank goodness he got his central nervous system organized and has since been transformed into a very agreeable baby. It's lucky for him because he doesn't have much of a choice with two not-very-older sisters. In August we found him securely strapped in his bouncy seat gnawing on a wedge of corned beef presumably launched by Lil from a nearby highchair. There were no witnesses willing to talk.

Lil (at almost two) has become quite a little person during the past year. Her enthusiasm for climbing is the reason our kitchen chairs are indefinitely locked in the dining room and her favorite activity is stuffing raisins (or dried apricots, Mr. Potato Head parts, etc.) down the heater's air intake vent while we're on the phone. Her favorite dinner is croutons and we're certain she considers ketchup a food group. As parents, Alan and I thought we'd never endorse a "favorite blankie" for any of our independent children, but we spent last Friday night in front of the washing machine supervising Lil on a stepstool watching THE chosen blanket go round-and-round to rid it of an unmistakable barf-smell. She has also started to talk and her first sentences were quite telling:

Sentence #1: See bug. (A comment about our superior housekeeping skills. A tattle.)

Sentence #2: Sister bites. (Another tattle. It didn't take a forensic dentist to figure out who was responsible for the three sets of teeth marks on her back.)

But in Jen's defense, it is difficult to live with a toddler. A few weeks ago while we were in the kitchen she and Lil went into the powder room together - alone. There was silence, then sounds of an obvious struggle before a sobbing scream from Jen. "I want to flush it! IT'S MY POOP!!!!"

While she wasn't enjoying the company of her sister, Jen had quite a busy year. She had her first experience with organized sports on a honest-to-goodness soccer team. In the first game she scored her first goal – but in the game taking place on the adjacent field. It wouldn't have been notable except for her NFL-quality victory dance that had the sidelines of both teams in hysterics. We think that Jen is also loving pre-school. She bounces out of the playground each day and announces "I had fun!" Then when asked what she did her response is "Nothing. I don't remember." We're going to be in trouble when she's a real teenager! And trying to be responsible parents, we spent the first half of the year trying to teach Jen her address and phone number. She spent the first half of the year insisting that she lived with Sandy in Texas where she worked. When pressed for details she'd explain that her job was making crabby patties with Spongebob. It was a powerful and frightening testament to the power of Nickelodeon. And she is, shall we say, quite chatty. Living with Jen is like being on the receiving end of a firehose that sprays words from dawn until about ten o'clock at night. We're grateful that she, at least, has a sense of humor. Absolutely disgusted, she told Lil "Just get a LIFE!" And the first thing out of her mouth one morning was "Do we have to stay home today and take care of the two stinky babies?"

Alan and I are doing well and as always are grateful to get a moment of peace here and there. As a person, I can be summarized by the contents of my purse: a tin of Altoids, a plastic dinosaur with a chewed tail, one cup of pulverized Cheeze-Its and no cash. And it is hard not to read anything into Alan's excited reaction when UPS delivered his new foul-weather winter suit. Any outing away from the chaos, even to snowblow the driveway in frigid weather, is welcome.

Jake continues to be the source of much of our sanity even though he had a difficult winter ending in surgery to have his ACL repaired. The surgery was uneventful, but to make a very long story short, the bonnet he wore to protect his stitches rubbed a sore on his hock. He then proceeded to eat quite a bit of his own leg. We know Jake will eat just about anything, but even we were impressed that he'd eat meat that was still attached to him.

Last month we added another member to our "herd." Isold is an adorable Icelandic mare who is powerful, talented, and now in charge of the barn. It was fascinating to watch her make her move. A little kicking, chasing, squealing, nipping, and it was little Isold first in line for dinner, with Blakkur and Brandur waiting a respectful distance behind. You go girl!

So now that the net weight of the family has increased by almost 1000 pounds, our warm, fuzzy moments are warmer and fuzzier and the breakdowns in order and the social structure are much more dramatic. And, as always, if you are in the area we'd love for you to join us. Have a wonderful holiday season!

Best Wishes,

Alan, Alyse, Jen, Lil,
Zach, Jake, Blakkur,
Brandur, & Isold

HAPPY HOLIDAYS 2004

We're coming to you this year from Galway, NY – our new place in the world. Having decided that we really love Upstate NY and would like to stay, we took the plunge, bought the back end of a family-owned piece of property, and are building a house. So, we spent the first part of the year sprucing up our former house so that we could convince someone to buy it. Next, we spent much of the summer figuring out how to get rid of as much stuff as possible because it was apparent that we hadn't thrown anything away since the 80's. Then we put what was left into a 16' horse trailer and hauled it across town. It was a different experience from our previous company-sponsored moves where our biggest concern was getting reimbursed for lunch. We'd forgotten what it was like to carry our own couch. And here we are in a borrowed mid-1800's farmhouse with everything we own in the basement under tarps. All in all, it was a cathartic start-from-scratch kind of experience. Thus far, all we have to show for our efforts is a driveway, culvert, basement, and plenty of mud. But we do have a vision and we're confident that with elbow grease and grass seed we can create a great place. We think that the courage/insanity/chutzpah to make this change came from the realization that our life with kids makes the 3 stooges look like an organized bunch with a plan.

Our children are really growing fast. Jen, Lil, and Zach are now 5, 3 & 1. They ensure that we don't take anything in our lives too seriously. Nick is very fast & his current obsession is turning off the dishwasher while it's in-progress and climbing to the highest point in every room. Lil is equally obsessed with "snips" and we are amazed at the power of child-safe scissors in her hands. Reams of paper have been reduced to confetti, holes created in several outfits, dolly hair chopped and stuffed animal fur buzzed. The final straw was the day we found her prized scissors along with her bangs stashed under the couch as if no one would notice she was practically bald. Now the snips are on the top of the fridge indefinitely.

Jen lives out of a dictionary of her own creation. This year she insisted that boy ballerinas are "baleroons" and that when you throw up at home you are "homesick" (as opposed to carsick, we assume). When startled, she says that her "heart is beeping really fast" and when cooking this summer she "dropped the can opener and almost chipped my foot." It makes perfect sense to us & maybe we all could learn something from her.

Lil and Jen are an amazing mix of maturity and competence but at the same time constant reminders of the fact that their reality is not the same as ours. Lil asked for help yesterday when she was playing games on www. nickjr.com "Mom, could you help me? I got into something and I logged off." But at the same time she is convinced that Alan's boss is "the e-mail," and when I told her that Alan was working she immediately asked "On the railroad?" And I recently had the pleasure of a 2AM in-depth discussion with Jen reassuring her that no, I was not a robot and that yes, I would have told her if I were. And among our group, justice continues to be swift. Lil recently ran screaming into the kitchen followed by a decidedly smug Jen who calmly explained "I had to Mom. Lil showed me her butt so I bit her on the can." Can you blame her? Their lack of adherence to social convention is so refreshing to us and underscores that if we don't want the answer, then we shouldn't ask the question.

This year's favorite's are:

What do you want in your princess thermos to take to school? Coffee. (Jen)

What do you want for breakfast? Rigatoni. (Lil)

What do you want to do today? Pick up golf. (Jen, in February with 2 feet of snow on the ground)

Nick's answer to everything is "NO! NO! NO!"

Aside from providing comic relief, the children have given us some great ways to spend our time. Alan has spent weekend mornings sifting through contents of the vacuum cleaner bag to retrieve microscopic plastic body parts from the Operation game and figuring out how (and in what configuration) to reattach the keys to his computer after Lil picked them all off. I recently had the task of getting several rolls of tape off of Lil after Jen had mummified her from head to toe. We were unsuccessful at scrubbing green magic marker out of Nick's nose after he colored the inside (we think up to his brain) of his nostrils.

But Alan is in heaven at our new place – it was the perfect excuse to get more tools and a bigger tractor with all the attachments. Thus far, the brush-hog has been his favorite with the chainsaw being a close second. Any doubt where the genes for "Lil the Snipper" come from? And our animals are fine. Other than Jake spending the 1st week of last year with a homemade duct-tape bandage on a claw that wouldn't stop bleeding he continues to be the king of our house. And the horses are fine, too, and continue to be the most consistently cooperative members of our family. Happy Holidays and New Year to all.

Love Always,

Alan & Alyse, Jen, Lil Scissorhands, & Zach
    Plus the ever wonderful Jake
    Blakkur, Brandur and Isold

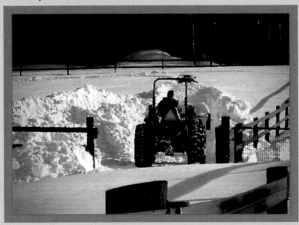

Happy Holidays 2005

Well, what can we say....we are still in Galway, New York in a borrowed farmhouse and our stuff is still in the basement under tarps, probably moldy by now. But since we haven't needed it in a year and a half, it can't be too important. This explains and/or excuses the enclosed family photo which honestly is this year's best. As you may have noticed, the children are dressed up for Halloween. Jen is in her stained fairy suit from two years ago since she didn't like this year's costume. Lil has torn up her pom-poms all over the kitchen before we left the house, and Zach feels confident in the dog suit (the 4th year in a row it's been worn) because after a quick peek in the mirror wearing the new skeleton costume, he scared himself so badly that he refused to wear it for the main event. They're armed with Easter basket buckets because their pumpkins are somewhere in tarp-land and we couldn't bear to add additional plastic pumpkins to our life. We are on the way to the mall where country kids trick-or-treat in freezing weather and are posed in the parking lot of the Residence Inn where my parents spent the fall after their condo was flooded by the drunk dude upstairs having fun with the building sprinkler system. So, to sum it up, our final answer is... 'No our house ain't done yet!'

Aside from the outward patheticness, it has been a good year. It began with a January call from "Guiding Eyes for the Blind" saying they had the perfect dog for us to adopt. Knowing that we wanted another lab, we put our name on the waiting list in 2000 with the idea that a reject guide dog is like a kid who flunks out of MIT - still pretty smart. So the next day Scott drove home with Vito, a huge, loveable 3 $\frac{1}{2}$ year old black lab who'd spent the last 2 years as a working guide. His owner's desk job kept the mega-energetic Vito sitting still for too long each day. Vito is beyond a Velcro dog and it has been really interesting getting to know him. It was obvious from the beginning that Vito's approach made perfect sense for a dog used to living with a blind guy ..."As long as I'm quiet, I can do anything I want because you can't see me." He began his new life with a celebratory blueberry pie off of the counter. No noise, no mess... no pie. Vito's enthusiasm for eating inspired them both to gain a quick 15 pounds each and like the rest of us they're now dieting and still haven't lost a single pound. But we all (especially Jake) love him although the dog fur problem in the house is out of control.

Jen, now 6, spent the summer losing teeth (pretty much all of them) and had to face the biggest disappointment of her life with the cancellation of her birthday bash due to fever and vomiting. But she rebounded in time to start kindergarten, coming home the first day just amazed by the "giant nugget" (aka chicken patty sandwich) that was served in the cafeteria. Zach at age 2 has become increasingly destructive, smashing three windowpanes this year, one as the sun went down on a -10F night. But he has shown us his softer side as well as he spent quite a bit of the year obsessed with the video, "I Want to be a Ballerina." Several times each week he dons a leotard and slippers to perform with his sisters. We have the home movies to prove it. And Lil, just turning 4, gets the "golden tongue" award this year. Her sometimes obnoxious and sometimes clever best are:

"It's been grassified." (what happens to a carpet when a dog barfs grass on the rug)

"Don't smash them they're just Home Flies" (summertime black flies in the house that don't bite)

"Because I have a lot of air in my mouth." (why she's so noisy)

"Mom, could you please get off your can and get me a drink?" (requesting a beverage with dinner)

"I need some time alone, away from this place." (why she should get a solo visit to her grandparents' house)

Alan spent much of this year outside and is quickly becoming a gentleman farmer. He built horse stalls, renovated pastures, and became a fence expert after pounding the 300th fence post into the ground. He also spent a lot of time on his backhoe digging trenches. Alyse is looking forward to a new kitchen after the last year and a half of cooking with the electric skittle, hot pot and bar-b-cue. Our college-style pans are beginning to disintegrate because of overuse and grilling while wearing a parka and snow boots is quickly losing its charm.

As a family, we hope to be back in action shortly.

We wish you all a wonderful holiday and a very happy 2006.

"The Family Funny Farm"

Alan, Alyse, Jen, Lil, Zach, Jake, Vito, Brandur, Blakkur and Isold

HAPPY HOLIDAYS 2006

We are very relieved that we're finally in our new house. Finishing it was a major fire drill - sort of like Extreme Home Makeover goes to boot camp. We moved in the last of our stuff literally at the stroke of midnight on New Year's Eve. Needless to say, this was a little too symbolic and we could have lived without the drama of it all. Alan and I are in total agreement that the building process was by far the most stressful thing we've ever done. Part of the "challenge" was that we weren't able to hook up to any city utilities except for power. We began the project cheerfully, picking out paint colors and faucets, but by the end realized most of our time was spent becoming experts on septic design, well drilling, lightning rods and back-up generators. So we greeted 2006 entirely wiped out – both in spirit and in bank account. We spent the spring recovering without much furniture, and not really caring, while we watched our grass seed germinate.

Nevertheless, we were forced to address the mud-around-the-swingset issue. After soil-stabilization fabric, six inches of sand followed by six inches of pea gravel, it was really eye-opening to shop around for something to surround it with. We found that because we live near the quarries in upstate New York, it's significantly less costly to border a swingset area with granite blocks than to use the molded plastic designed for that purpose. The only downside is that (for those of you who haven't had the pleasure of such a project) rocks weigh A LOT - they're so heavy that two pallets maxed out the horse trailer – granite per cubic foot weighs much more than ponies. After multiple trips to the quarry, Alan finally finished. We calculated that this project and a flagstone path leading to it meant moving just under 23,000 lbs of rock. This is certainly why people hire landscaping crews.

There were also some important lessons we learned early this year:

If you leave plenty of nesting material in your Suburban (Pull-Up training pants, emergency toilet paper) and deliver food daily (Cheerios, French Fries) mice will build themselves a fabulous nest under the front seat.

If you do 20 loads of laundry in a single day (YeeHa! No more laundromats!) your well pump will suck up mud and turn your water black for weeks.

If you invite children to your house for a playdate, make sure their moms don't mind being towed out of a snow bank after failing to navigate your driveway.

Be nice to the Time-Warner guy because you don't know how long he'll be stuck in the same snow bank.

Burn piles that fit into a 55 gallon drum are considerably safer than burn piles the size of a small house. After an emergency trip to the barber to trim the fuzzies off of his hair, eyebrows and eyelashes, Alan will never again use gasoline to start a bonfire - KABOOM!

The kids are really great. Jen is in 1st grade and is the proud owner of a set of braces after a routine x-ray at the dentist came out looking like an L.A.-style traffic jam. Lil is in her final year of pre-school and is continuing to learn how the world works. She was absolutely shocked when it came out in conversation that there were actually dead people under those pretty rocks (some with flags!) in the graveyard across from the school. She also suggested that artists should be called "professional colorers." And Zach is the one we almost pulled out of the 3-year old pre-school class before it even began. "No way he'll be ready." Believe it or not, he's turned out to be the best one of the bunch. We think he lacks the girls' sophistication to stage an "I'm being abandoned" leg-grabbing melodrama.

We continue to find the "Nature vs. Nurture" debate fascinating and now that the kids are bunking separately in their own rooms, it has become even more apparent that Nature wins. Lil will lie in bed for the better part of an hour with her eyes open and then present herself downstairs fully dressed (socks and all) buttoning her sweater, hair combed and lip-gloss on. On the other hand, Zach crashes his way down like a drunken sailor weaving and hanging onto the railing. We're surprised he hasn't fallen down the stairs but grateful he actually gets out of bed to use the potty.

Vomit seems to make a cameo appearance in all of our end-of-the-year holiday ramblings and this year is no exception. Only the cast and the setting changes. This year's episode stars Zach and is set on Alan's birthday on a family drive to the outlet mall to buy him new jeans (already a pathetic story). It continues with Zach exploding all over himself as we are driving north (there's no good place to pull over north of Saratoga). Cut to us giving him a complete overhaul with baby wipes outside a gas station on a windy 30-degree day. Follow with the discovery that we had no spare clothes and no way to rehab the contaminated outfit. Close the scene with us wrapping the star (except for his head) in a Glad trash bag and strapping the whole bundle back into what Zach now refers to as the "puke-seat." There are no plans to release a soundtrack. Happy Birthday, Alan!

The horses and dogs are enjoying room to roam and grass to eat and we've found that since we now have wood floors all we have to do on a windy day is open a few windows and all of the dog fur will sweep itself into a ball in the corner. Nice. And at the end of this month we're adding to our menagerie four pregnant Icelandic ewes (yes sheep!) When settling the livestock question we were looking for a species that would be able to thrive in the cold, was unlikely to trample a kid, could double as a 4-H project and could provide chops. In preparation for their arrival Alan has built adorable movable sheep-shacks for them and we've had the pleasure of joining the USDA Scrapie Program. We will let you know how the sheep project evolves...

From all of us, we wish you the best in 2007!

Love, Alyse, Alan, Jen, Lil, and Zach, Blakkur, Brandur, Isold, Jake & Vito

HAPPY HOLIDAYS 2007

Greetings from our family to yours. We hope this letter finds you all well.

Winter came first and this year was ushered in as the "Year of the Wood Router." Alan had the liberating experience of being able to write anything he wanted on whatever he wanted and hang it wherever he pleased. For a while we were petrified that we'd come home and find our house labeled "stove," "mudroom," "potty," but thankfully things stayed outside and we are happy to say that you will NEVER get lost in the Family Woods because our trails are better-marked (and more artistically) than the trails in Yosemite. Alan had to scrub the sawdust off in time to make a week-long January meeting in Dallas. Usually these meetings represent a quiet time for the rest of us, but this time picture a split/screen. On the left you have Alan watching the weather channel on the hotel treadmill trying to work off a steakhouse event from the evening before, and on the right you have the rest of us (Alyse, the 3 kids, 2 dogs, 3 horses and 4 pregnant sheep) watching a big, big storm head our way. It wasn't too bad at first because being holed up with a barnful of hay and about 4 dozen boxes of Girl Scout cookies wasn't too challenging. After Mother Nature dumped about 4 feet of snow, our neighbor Mike (aka Buckwheat), after a few days of seeing no evidence of life coming out of our driveway came to our rescue with a New York State issued snowplow (literally) and got us to the point where Alan wouldn't have to hoof it up the driveway. Five foot snowdrifts in "business casual" footwear would not have been fun. When Alan got home he went straight to work clearing more snow

and was going to do a good deed of clearing a little area for our flock to stand in so they could exit the barn for the first time in a week. To make a long story as short as possible, the horses got out (gate-operator error) and after almost a week of being cooped up behind the barn in a snowbank, they were more than happy to take themselves out for a little exercise. You haven't lived life until you have tried to follow Icelandic horses up a hill through several feet of snow. It took the golf cart, snowmobile, tractor, every neighbor on our street and a bucket of grain to retrieve them from the hill across and down the street about a mile away. And it was clearly their choice to get caught.

The icing on the cake happened when Alan went to retrieve his abandoned equipment from the snowbank on the side of our country road. He was greeted by the local sheriff saying, "Hey, Mister ... your snowmobile isn't registered." All Alan could say was, "I know, but please let me tell you about my day....." "No problem sir, just get it off the road." He spent the next day delivering pies to all the people whose yards we traversed and who (in the finest Galway tradition) came out to greet us in Carharts ready to lend a helping hand.

Spring came along and we continued our education with some hands-on training in the wonderful world of sheep obstetrics. To make another very long and convoluted story short, 3 of our ewes gave birth easily to 7 lambs amongst them but one got herself in trouble. Poor Jessie had a difficult triplet-birth and after a fairly gory 3 am scene in the barn, we ended up with a healthy ram lamb, a stillborn, and a spotted ewe lamb who wasn't doing well at all. Jessie came through like a champ and took care of her first baby but understandably decided baby #3 wasn't worth the trouble since it wasn't bouncing up to nurse like the others. But after a while under the hairdryer, baby #3 perked up but her mom was definitive, a no-go.

Alan and I became parents of a newborn all over again. The hands-down best gift ever for our kids was them waking up with the most adorable black and white lamb living in the house. They instantly named her Princess. Princess has only recently figured out that she is a sheep. She began life thinking she was a dog and had a grand time playing with the kids/dogs in the backyard and in the house if the kids put a diaper on her. She rode around on the golf cart, hiked in the woods and took a particular liking to butting heads with the tetherball. She visited nursery school, rode around in the back of the car and happily played the role of our "demo-lamb. We finally banished her to the pasture with her kind when we got fed up with the 3am feed-me-foghorn (not a cute baa at all) and irreparable damage to my attempt at petunias. I never thought it possible that our home would be vandalized by a lamb.

Summer soon followed and it turned into the season of bushless landscaping. Let me explain. After much thought and debate we decided that while the retaining wall is needed in front of our house, the project was quite a bit above our ability level, there was no reason why the back patio shouldn't be a DIY project for Alan with me designing the pattern for the stone (12 different sizes) and my dad providing the engineering consult for drainage and the concrete forms for the stairstep underlayment. It seemed beyond ridiculous to pay someone else to put rocks on the ground. And heck, since we were getting such a good deal by doing it ourselves, we figured we could make it a big patio (say, 1,700 sq ft). Well, after close to 100,000lbs. of palletted bluestone had been offloaded and neatly lined up behind the house

←TO THE BACK 20

(again, thanks to Buckwheat-with-his-own-forklift), we realized that once again we had begun a project that was way above our heads. Let's just say that after going through 9 truckloads of crushed stone, 2 trucks of stone dust, 3 diamond blades (oh yes, there was a lot of stone cutting involved), 2 visits by the big concrete truck, several reams of graph paper, 2 pairs of work shoes, many gloves, all the skin on the tips of Alan's fingers and 2 weeks worth of vacation days, we now have a patio that looks like a 2-tiered gray tennis court. Even though it turned out the way we planned it, we will NOT be doing that again anytime soon.

That being the main event of the summer we were more than ready to start the fall school routine with the kids. It's nice to have an older, experienced sibling (Jen) to give a nervous kindergartener (Lil) confidence on the first day of school. While we were making small talk at the bus stop Jen asks in a very condescending tone "Lil, does mom have to follow the bus to make sure you go in and don't hide in the bushes all day?" Jen seems to have forgotten the principal-escort that got her to her kindergarten classroom everyday until Thanksgiving. But we're not feeling so bad as Lil is quick to offer words of wisdom and confidence to Zach ranging from the fairly comforting ... "You know Zachy, sometimes you're the windshield and sometimes you're the bug..." to the passive aggressive, "Zach, you're dumb but we love you anyway." Thankfully Zach remains blissfully unaware of anything but trucks. We think it must be a defense mechanism to avoid being driven insane by his older sisters.

So the morals to our year's stories are...

#1: Gates are 100% effective when they are closed and absolutely useless when they are open.

#2: Keep the sheep in the barn or pasture if you value your sleep or decorative landscaping.

#3: Working with stone in the heat of August is miserably hard work and explains why professionals charge a lot to do it for you.

So although Alan's anxiety level is at an all-time high with "23 mouths to feed and at least a dozen more expected in April" we are keeping him calm by reminding him that by this time next year the grass-eating majority will hopefully be feeding us.

As always, if you are ever in the area we'd love for you to join us. Have a wonderful holiday season and a terrific 2008!

Best Wishes,

Alan, Alyse, Jen, Lil, Zach, Jake, Vito, Blakur, Brandur, Izzy and the 13 pregnant sheep

Happy Holidays 2008

We're coming to you in the midst of this year's barf-o-rama, i.e., life in the petri-dish of school age kids. As of now Jen is on the road to recovery after about a hundred trips to the loo, Lil is passed out on the couch sleeping it off and Zach "Iron-Gut" Fisher is marching around with a bucket, anticipating the inevitable. We're thankful for all of the beautiful snapshots of happy families we've received this year – it gives us hope.

But aside from the current atmosphere of good cheer in our home, 2008 has been an agreeable year. It began with countless trips to Ski Venture so the kids could learn to ski. Lest you have images of Vail-style resorts, gondolas and professional instructors, I must remind you that the official motto on their T-Shirts is "Ski Venture - We Run on Duct Tape." Our hill is nine miles away and open 24 hours a day by virtue of the fact that you undo the chain at the road, you unlock the padlock on the hut and you start up the tows which are powered by a recycled and brilliantly reconfigured 1950's pickup. If you want to turn on the floodlights at 3am, it's your own business. The giant clotheslinesque assembly is propped up by telephone poles and will haul anyone with the strength to hang on to the top of a surprisingly steep hill in under 20 seconds. Thus, the duct tape. No pair of man-made gloves can withstand the friction.

Our kids made amazing progress because there are no lift lines and they can ski as fast and wherever they want. They're anxiously awaiting our first big storm and Ski Venture is ready for another season. Alan knows because he drove our tractor over to brush hog the hill while the Cub Scouts re-roofed the outhouse. But at $60 per year per family, it truly is a local gem.

As the snow melted, two of our spring lambs took up residence in our foyer. This year we had dog crates set up for our bottle babies, "Lambie" (white) and "Blackie" (black).

Blackie was the product of a delivery assisted by our neighbor Buckwheat because Scott was out of town. Always the Renaissance man, Buckwheat (last summer's forklift hero and the blizzard rescuer from the year before) was most gracious about putting aside his welding project to provide an obstetrical assist at a moment's notice. Six months later Blackie's fleece went on to win a blue ribbon at the NY Sheep and Wool Festival. Needless to say, Blackie has now qualified as a permanent resident here.

In June, Lambie and Blackie joined the other 14 lambies in the pasture before we (and I use "we" loosely giving myself a lot of credit) began hauling home bushes. Our West Coast friends don't appreciate the "strike while the iron is hot" mentality of shopping for landscape plants in the Northeast. The snow melts, the mud dries up, and Lowe's has daylilies, or lilacs once. I mean ONCE and if you miss the window of opportunity, you're out of luck because by July the garden center is being restocked with snowblowers. Alan spent a week furiously planting perennials and we are patiently waiting and hoping that they will survive the winter. Spring will tell us if the ripped ligament in Alan's knee was worth it.

September came and with it Zach's foray into the world of public education. Our expectations were low because he'd had no interest in how to hold a pencil, write his name, or any of the other skills used to predict success in Kindergarten. But low and behold – a miracle has happened and now we have a kid who's so proud of his work that he insists on unpacking his backpack in the car on the way home to show off his creations. He even asked, "Does this make me artable?" after putting some serious effort into his latest craft project. He's a great example of our tax dollars at work.

His other accomplishment was being the "first kid in the pond" at the fishing derby at the Adirondack Museum. Kids were given the assignment of catching all of the trout from the museum's pond so they could drain it for winter. They were incredibly excited because these trout had been fed by the visitors all summer and ranged in size from 6 inches to 2 feet and hadn't been fed in days. Even though catching a fish was a sure thing, Zach went in (all the way in) with his first cast and had to do the demoralizing march, squishing back through the gift shop past the other fisherman kids signing in... for a long walk back to the car for dry clothes. The whole thing would have been much more entertaining if the air temperature had been above freezing.

So, as winter begins, the kids are embroiled in indoor soccer, Jen is preparing to be part of the recorder brigade at the school holiday concert, and Alan is debating when to put the chains on his tractor tires for some serious snow plowing.

Wishing you the best in 2009!

Alan, Alyse, Jen (9), Lil (7), Zach (5), Jake (12), Vito (6) and all 25 critters

Happy Holidays 2009

One morning in the 2nd week of Dec, during our pre-dawn coffee, Alan and I had our annual discussion about the holiday letter. This chat is predictably precipitated by the timely, post-Thanksgiving receipt of gorgeous family snapshots from efficient friends wishing us Yuletide cheer from warm places. As typical of these conversations Alan was bemoaning that we had absolutely nothing, especially nothing good to report while I insisted that we just needed to think harder. If Seinfield could write a decade worth of shows about "nothing," then we could certainly generate a page-long holiday letter. Our only option was an anti-letter, while cathartic to write, might be taken as an ungrateful and sadistic way to celebrate the spirit of the season

<u>Kid Review</u> As they grow the kids are increasingly independent. Jen has started packing her own lunch which usually includes "loose" slices of bread and a tub of chicken salad so she can make her sandwich "on site." Lil has spent the last few weeks knitting like a madman – and the attention to detail that allows her to focus for hours at a time caused her to be horrified at the "inappropriate" museum statues (priceless, 2000 year old naked Greek and Romans, many missing appendages). Zach continues to remind us to not ask questions if we don't want answers. He brought home a feel-good Thanksgiving writing/illustrating assignment from school, "If I were a turkey..." His comment? "If I were a turke....I wud hid in a tree so I wudn't get shot." The illustration was accurate. And a few weeks ago we had quite a scare as Zach woke up in a puddle of blood...until we traced the blood from his shoulder down his arm to his wrist, index finger and then back up to his crusty left nostril. Case closed.

<u>Dog Report</u> This summer, after almost 13 years, we lost Jake to old age– we miss him terribly, but on a positive note, our name came up on the Guiding Eyes waiting list again.

We adopted Weston, a fussy cat-dog who prances and bounces, doesn't get his feet wet, who flunked out for "work avoidance." Hmmm...perfect for around here. Barely more than a puppy, he made himself right at home by eating Zach's down comforter with Zach sleeping in it (a shocking way to wake up...feathers everywhere... "Mom am I in trouble?"), the arm cover of the living room couch, and the legs of the dining room table and chair look like they've been attacked by beavers. In almost a year we've never heard him bark but he drools like a basset hound when we make dinner. He is absolutely hysterical.

<u>Livestock Update</u> Spring marked the arrival of about 30 lambs which now populate local backyards and freezers and will be followed by another 30 or so this April. No sheep lived in the house this year so we are making progress on that front.

This summer marked the start of the Family's chicken project. Alan finally cracked and ordered a coop for Mother's Day. It arrived in 5 very large and very flat boxes ("I ordered it because I didn't want to BUILD you a chicken coop!") But it snapped together looking very much like it was made by LittleTykes (you know, those preformed plastic picnic tables and playhouses), and is actually called an "Eglu." An embarrassingly suburban addition to our farm, it's on wheels so you can move it around because the option is cleaning the coop which is most unpleasant. The chickens arrived by mail and ordered online from www.mypetchicken.com. They were mailed the day they hatched, because when a chick hatches (this was news to us, too) they suck the remaining yolk up into their bodies which buys them enough time for Express Mail to work. We unpacked 3 ordinary red hens, 3 black and white speckled hens, and 6 gorgeous fuzzy-faced "Easter-eggers" in all the colors of the rainbow who are known for laying blue and green eggs – no roosters. To make a long story short, the 3 ordinary red hens give us 3 giant brown eggs every morning by 6AM sharp and they are so tame you can carry them around like footballs under your arm. The 3 speckled hens give us 3 small cream-colored eggs sometime each day and are almost as friendly as the red hens. The 6 colorful hens who lay colorful eggs? Zip, zilch, nada. And when they escape from the coop you can't catch them. Pretty is as pretty does, but we will wait until next spring before plugging in the crock pot. Vito is especially thrilled with the hens as they provide a continual supply of chicken poo, his new favorite farm-fresh snack.

Equipment Inventory New this year are several rolls of electronet fencing and a boat.

Parent Chronicle We've been fine but a bit busy...one day a few weeks ago we had a day which was notably ridiculous... After putting kids 1 and 2 on the bus I went for my appt at the neuro-opthomologist 45 min south while Alan was on a mandatory morning teleconference. That wouldn't have been a big deal but they had dilated my eyes, stranding me there while kid 3 was waiting at home for a ride to the pediatrician for a throat culture. And immediately after his teleconference (assuming I brought the truck home) Alan needed to haul the 3 pigs (waiting in our trailer parked in the driveway next door) to the "processor" across town. They were parked there because if they were parked in our driveway for any length of time they would be claimed, named, and become permanent residents of

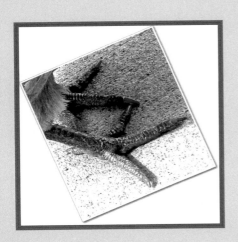

the backyard, which was NOT the plan. Oh, and the rental company car needed to be returned in Saratoga and the repaired company car picked up an hour south. And kids 1 and 2 were picked up from school at 3:15. We got it done but it was an obvious pizza night.

PS In an addendum to last year we found that the best time to put the chains on the tractor is on a sunny day before you really need them. It's the end of December and they're still not on.

Happy and Healthy 2010 to all!

Happy Holidays 2010

2010 was a very good year for all of us here at the Family Funny Farm. We joke that while Alan is joining the 21st century with Apple TV and terabytes, I'm regressing toward the 1700's with a brand new spinning wheel and mountains of fleece. Our flock still easily meets our demands for both fiber and chops but is competing for space in the freezer with the great tomato harvest of 2010. Following 2009's miserable tomato year, this summer turned into tomato hell. Cute, almost decorative, baskets turned into five-gallon paint buckets unceremoniously lined up in the mudroom waiting their turn. After simmering almost 100 quarts of sauce and filling every car that ventured up our driveway with baskets of the dammed fruit, we'll never plant as many tomatoes again.

As if trying to outdo the tomatoes, the chickens started laying eggs in earnest and amused us as they paraded about the yard. Their eggs had brilliant orange yolks, probably from eating all of our hostas as fast as they sprouted. They answered the question, "How fast can a dozen chickens eat a 50lb bag of freshly spread premium weed-free grass seed?" The answer: eight minutes. Their days of freedom became numbered when they learned to loiter by the back door where the kids would toss treats, and anyone who has ever known a chicken knows you don't want them spending too much time hanging around begging like seagulls at a picnic. To make matters worse, they were more than a match for Alan's flower beds, flinging mulch everywhere as they scratched for bugs. Therefore, the entire flock was corralled inside a fence except Teresa (named after Mother Teresa). She knows how to fly. Flapping her wings like a madman, she barely clears the fence and has the run of the yard all day before putting herself to bed on a front porch rocking chair. Every night, I'd scoop her off of her roost and return her to her coop. Having been on the loose all day we never knew if/where/when she was laying eggs, until Zach and his cousin happened upon a cache of more than 20 blue eggs under a bush. Teresa enjoyed her role as our $2 pseudo-parrot, riding around on shoulders, coming when called, and joining us around the fire pit every night we're there. Teresa and her girlfriends have even provided us with some brilliant parenting insights. There's a "chicken bucket" in the kitchen to collect scraps of every kind that are happily recycled into eggs. It was a lightbulb parenting moment when I said "Don't you DARE put that crap in there – we can't feed them THAT!" "THAT" was Zach's leftover lunch - DUH! So now we try a little harder to live up to the "chicken bucket" standard of healthy living. Who knew chickens are so cool?

As summer began, Jen and Lil signed up for 4H dog training, figuring it would be a snap because of older and more advanced students. Not so. While the girls attended the dog-free orientation, the dogs spent the hour in the car shredding phone books and soccer shoes. Then, during the first dog-day, Vito after many years of leash-free living, completely disregarded the kid at the end of the leash, worked the crowd like a celebrity, inspired anarchy among the other students, peed on Jen's foot and received the instruction that he show up next week wearing a spiked collar. Weston just whined and refused to sit. Lil and Jen were mortified and have been invited to repeat the course in 2011. The rest of the summer we operated a de facto B&B until our well (literally) ran dry.

As September drew near, Zach started taking an interest in his appearance, and after being presented with back-to-school toiletries (toothpaste, mouthwash, etc.) came down on the first day of 2nd grade with hair slicked, shirt neatly tucked, a bloody face and vehement denials that he had shaved. Not good, but at least it wasn't picture day. He's becoming more grown-up all the time and recently told us, "Stop giving me all these things to do! You're stretching me out!" Also, Lil lost two teeth with braces still attached and then had the chutzpah to argue that she deserved a bonus from the Tooth Fairy. But we quickly nixed that by telling her if she wasn't careful she'd owe us a hundred bucks for each tooth with expensive hardware attached. The other notable event of early fall was doing back-to-school shopping and discovering that Jen is taller than I am and also wears size 8 sneakers.

We've just returned from an out-of-character (pun absolutely intended) experience - a week at Disney World. Yup, yes we did. For me, who doesn't like crowds or hot weather, I can tell you that I was not expecting much. We found that planning this trip was a lot like being pregnant - everyone has her own experience to share, which was appreciated because all we knew was that Mickey lived there. Two tidbits that stood out immediately were: 1.) December is great because of the gorgeous holiday decorations and 2.) There are now "apps" to help navigate the horrendous crowds. You've GOT to be kidding me...APPS? Thankfully, it was Mother Nature to our rescue. When we arrived, the grounds looked remarkably like Upstate NY - until a closer inspection revealed that instead of snow, giant white tarps covered the billions of poinsettias to protect them from the frost. The wind chill of 17 degrees gave us Upstate New York farm-style early risers, the advantage. Screaming squadrons of 4-year olds, frozen into their princess costumes were strollered out of the park in droves. Even the monorail stopped ("It's too cold for the hydraulics."), allowing us, ever fleet and flexible, to jump in a cab and race to take the most memorable picture of the trip, a family photo with the backdrop being a totally empty parking lot at EPCOT. We really are the Griswolds and we really were the first civilians there. In fact, we have a similar picture from each of the four Disney parks and as a result of our early arrivals, we were able to visit each theme park in its entirety in six hours or less. Other than one incident of inter-sibling violence in the "It's a Small World" queue and another when Jen's elbow bloodied Zach's nose as they danced through a fountain, things went smoothly. Lil did lose one day to illness but is now recognized as the only one of our kids ever to barf in the lobby of the Grand Floridian Resort and Spa.

On the final day of our vacation our three kids had a giant pool, complete with a battalion of lifeguards and it's own waterslide entirely to themselves ALL day. The lifeguards were dressed for an Everest expedition complete with hats, gloves, and neck warmers to combat the cold snap while our children swam. While calling the kids out of the pool $\frac{1}{2}$ hour before the Magical Express (aka hotel bus) was due to whisk us to the airport, Alan (always, and by far, our most coordinated family member) ended up in the pool in his airport attire. Keep in mind that airport attire means outerwear anticipating a 10 degree arrival in Upstate NY, not flip-flops and shorts. Poolside, dripping and fully dressed. This would have been the most magical of moments to capture on camera. Alas, our camera had also fallen into the pool along with our cell phone, boarding passes and wallets. After assuring the horrified staff that this was hysterically funny, they admitted it was the best thing they'd witnessed all week.

So as we look back at the events of 2010, we're constantly reminded to appreciate the times of plenty, whether tomatoes or snow, and to do our best to laugh when we inevitably end up in the drink. Have a wonderful holiday season, and a happy and healthy 2011.

Best wishes to you all!

Alan, Alyse, Jen (11), Lil (9), Zach(7), Dogs, Horses, Sheep and Chickens

Happy Holidays 2011

The beginning of 2011 was delightfully uneventful – no driveway luge course, notable blizzards or animal drama. There was a lot of snow, but it was fluffy and easy to manage. For once, winter was what it was supposed to be, a time for the people and the land to rest. We have our fingers crossed for more of the same.

Alan spent the winter coming to grips with the fact that his ancient Craftsman lawn tractor had come to the end of its useful life. It was a hard pill to swallow and was only possible after looking back at the reams of repair receipts since it ate several $50 belts/month. Each mow invariably ended by towing the inoperable mower back to the garage. Not even the charming look of the bungee-cord-secured hood could buy it another summer. Now it's been relegated to the woods with the other abandoned pieces of equipment, our mechanical purgatory that I call the "scary area." But Alan managed to fill the hole in his heart with a landscaper quality zero-turn. After using at least two tanks of gas driving around before the grass started to grow, we've gotten our two-person-four-acre-mow-time down to under an hour of fun with no follow-up repair.

Touched by the Spirit of Spring, Zach took up woodworking by hauling anything he could muscle from the scrap pile in the woods to the area behind the garage. Pounding nails was so much fun that when he ran out of wood he continued driving nails into the stone driveway – roofing nails, framing nails, finish nails...and there were a zillion of them. This was all fun and games until one mysteriously ended up in the trailer tire. That spelled the end of "Do what you want–we live in the country." Finding and extracting gray nails from a gray driveway one by one was a tedious end to this project.

After the tomato tsunami of 2010, we approached the garden with too much hubris, thinking we'd be fine with a fifth of last year's harvest. With standing water in the vegetable garden until mid-May, we didn't bother to prepare the soil. We just planted the seeds, put the plants in the dirt, and were rewarded accordingly. You really do reap what you sow. Lesson learned. There's a reason they make rototillers and till-we-will in 2012. Although our garden was almost a total write-off, we made up for it by spending many mornings at a U-Pick blueberry patch around the corner. With forced child labor at 50 cents/bag (no stems or greens!) we were able to harvest enough for the winter.

Because of the endless rain, water was not in short supply above ground, but it certainly wasn't making it to our well. Wells are like roofs, septic systems, and moms. You don't notice them until they're gone and at that point everything grinds to a halt. When we got the official pump-test news that we were running on less than a third of a gallon per minute, we didn't know whether to be really bummed or give ourselves a gold star for being able to support 5 people, 2 horses, 2 dogs, 52 sheep and 12 chickens, even though our children considered a bathtub bath a luxury. After drilling a new well, we now have more and better water. It's a huge quality of life improvement and we can all take showers and fill the troughs on the same day we do laundry. Every load that doesn't come out the color of mud still feels like a small triumph.

Vito celebrated summer by eating the entire contents of the "chicken bucket" off of the counter. It would have been fine as we feed our chickens well, but it included nine corncobs from a family dinner the evening before. The X-ray looked exactly like you'd expect it to look after nine corncobs. But since he'd had all night to chew them thoroughly, guess what the solution was? He avoided surgery by downing about 30 Vaseline sandwiches. Seriously...Vaseline slathered on Wonderbread. Who knew? After several days of greasy corncob puree coming out of both ends he was back in action. But as a typical Lab, he didn't learn his lesson and celebrated Fall with Lil's Halloween candy, also pilfered at night. After making the unilateral decision that he'd used up his X-ray quota for the year, he responded by barfing up about 50 candy wrappers in the dining room while I was enjoying a rare cup of tea with a friend.

The kids? They're still around, although a little less since they're going to a new school. To make a very long story short and to avoid summarizing my six-page manifesto to the school board, they've joined the uniform-wearing ranks of private school kids. Argh. We've gotten over the trauma of dropping our babies off at the Park-n-Ride to catch the bus to Albany, although the irony of doing so after moving to the country to enjoy small-town life is absolutely not lost on us. School being an hour away is a definite game-changer. There's no longer an emergency drop-off service for band instruments or forgotten homework. Missing the bus has become a very big deal. One day Jen didn't move fast enough and was stranded in Albany with Lil and Zach heading north on the I-87 during rush hour. A complete fiasco. Their new orders are standard military, or Star Trek, depending on your inclination. As much as they'd love to, they must NEVER leave one of their own behind.

Their days are long but the school is good and offers them interesting opportunities. Gym classes use the school's ice rink and Lil is quite the picture sporting sparkling white figure skates on her feet and the required hockey helmet with full-face grill on her head, Hannibal Lecter on ice. The food is better too, but Zach's mandatory healthy snack ended up liquefied in his backpack during Thanksgiving vacation. It had been a banana.

The kids are learning a lot about personal responsibility. The aftermath of Jen's decision to eat three plates of fried clams at the lunchtime all-you-can eat buffet did not get her any sympathy at home. Meanwhile, we exist in a Bermuda Triangle. The vertices are Home, Albany Academy and the Orthodontist. And again, hubris has come to haunt us on that front as well. After the girls post-finger-sucking orthodontic disasters we thought we were in good shape with Zach. No thumb damage and what looked like a lot of room. We were shocked when the orthodontist (who now, after five years, is practically family) walked in with Zach's X-ray and summed it up. "Well, you didn't win the lottery with this one." Next year we'll let you know the outcome of the saga of Zach's impacted canines. Unfortunately, it will take a lot more to fix him than a loaf of Wonderbread and a tub of Vaseline.

We wish you a great holiday season and a healthy and happy 2012!

Much love from all of us (you're counted if you eat)

Alan, Alyse, Jen, Lil and Zach

Happy Holidays 2012

Each December, the first step before writing our holiday letter is to re-read past letters, both for inspiration and to make sure we aren't repeating ourselves. The photos remind us that our kids are still growing and look to be in reasonably good condition, and the stories within bring comfort that this year's litany of fiascos didn't compare with 2005. This is all fine, but there's a downside. The ill-fated burn pile that torched off Alan's eyebrows in the fall of 2006 was finally burned to the ground last week.... December of 2012. If it weren't in writing we'd convince ourselves it had only been gracing our yard for six months instead of six years. And as we read we can no longer dismiss gentle suggestions from loved ones to use larger font for our letter. Now in the 16th year of Alan,and my annual 27th birthday, we ourselves can't read our letters unless they're three feet away and every light in the house is on. 11pt font? Green? What happened to our X-Ray vision? So while we can't promise that we'll have more, or better, news to report, we will share it in 14pt black.

Watching the kids grow really drives home the point that time is marching on, and hopefully this will be the final year we give our entire flex spending account to the orthodontist. Zach is in 4th grade, transitioning from plastic toys to expensive electronics, but he'll still come downstairs and announce, "Mom, I don't know what happened, but I woke up covered in gum!" And this year was the last time we had a child in the school's Halloween Parade. I stood lined up and teary-eyed with the other parents. The kindergartners filed past as the most adorable fairies and cowboys; the 2nd graders were mostly Spidermen; but by the time the 4th graders appeared, they'd degenerated to looking like a bunch of hoodlums and hookers, so I didn't even bother to take a picture. Good riddance to the Halloween Parade.

Zach also faces real life choices. He succinctly summed up the Fundamental Consumer Problem when he lamented, "If I KNEW I wanted an iPod Touch, I wouldn't have spent all my money on Beyblades. It's NOT FAIR! They hadn't even been invented yet!!!!!" All I could think was, "Well...if I KNEW I had to send you to college, I wouldn't have bought all those fancy clothes and nights out on the town because I didn't even KNOW I was having YOU!" Live and learn.

Choices are tough for parents, too. For Christmas this year Zach wants either a parakeet or a James Bond video game. Hmmm...this now becomes our problem because one is clearly better for the kid and one is clearly easier for us. We have to admit if we ban the bird in favor of an electronic babysitter we're accepting responsibility for every poor choice he'll make for the rest of his life. One good choice this year was his interest in personal hygiene. After coming home from a friend's house smelling like the perfume aisle in Macy's, he explained that they "tried out" all the older brother's toiletries, and that now he was ready for deodorant. Hallelujah! He took a quick look at the selection in the grocery store and said, "It's not here," and led me to the cleaning product aisle where he announced, "That's it!" Febreeze. Wanting to confirm that it was the right scent, he tried it out then and there by squirting himself in the eye.

That incident was cleaning product déjà vu. It triggered memories of Lil's infamous playdate (I played the role of responsible adult) when the girls applied make-up. It was all fun and games until they came downstairs for a snack, all cleaned up. I asked how they removed the pounds of eye shadow and lipstick and Lil proudly said, "I used the baby wipes from your bathroom." She had scrubbed her guests' faces with Clorox wipes. It wasn't a proud parenting moment, phoning the other parents to be on the lookout for bleach burns on their childrens' faces. Luckily, no permanent damage was done and Lil, always a picture of humility, has grown into the self-proclaimed "Queen of Classroom Objects" in her Spanish class (el libro, la boligrafo, la tareja). I'm beginning to think we should all have titles.

But she, too, is starting to venture into the grown-up world, beginning with her cell phone. The idea was to use it for rides and to chit-chat with friends. No texting. When Alan questioned an extra $30 data charge on our monthly cell phone bill she was shocked. "I swear I didn't do it. I don't even know HOW to text!" The Verizon tech on the phone clarified, "Apparently you do. 48 times. Like yesterday at 4:02." Lesson learned. Don't lend your phone, every day, to someone on the bus who has a crush on a 5th grade boy and no cell phone of her own.

And Jen is doing really well, although she upped the ante in inter-sibling violence by being behind the wheel of a spectacular collision between our golf cart and Zach. She learned the lesson that, "But he didn't get out of the way!" is not an excuse for flattening him. Thank goodness for the grill that launched him to the relative safety of the landscape rocks. The frightening thing about this is that she is already 13, which means that she'll soon be driving a real car and we'll all need to stay off the roads until she learns to yield to pedestrians. We'll send out a global alert when that is imminent. But as life always provides balance, she was on the receiving end of quite a bit of physical punishment as the goalie for the JV soccer team. Playing against high schoolers who out-sized her was quite the experience. She ended up receiving a trophy at the sports banquet for her outstanding efforts – even though they never won a game. Let's just say that practically the only people that touched the ball this season were Jen and the opposing team, with Jen averaging around 50 saves per game. Dare we hope for better luck next year?

On the home front, our efforts to be a little more self-sufficient got off to an excellent start this spring. After our no-tillage-dry-well disaster last summer we were committed to nurturing the fruits of our earth. The Jolly Green Giant couldn't have done a better job until June. We tilled, we weeded, we watered and our garden was on the cusp of producing a farmer's market. Then the rain stopped. Completely. Soon, all over the neighborhood water trucks were filling up wells instead of pools. Not wanting to Darwin ourselves by growing irrigated vegetables during a drought using up our finite and uncertain amount of water, our tomatoes soon withered on the vine. We shall begin again next year.

The animals are doing well with the sheep being the only ones (again) paying their own way. The only problem is that somehow I ended up with four rams who are now in rut and doing their best to bash my barn to smithereens. They are called rams for a reason. Next winter I plan to have only one, so if anyone is interested in welcoming Vinnie, Prince or George to your backyard or freezer, please let me know. The chickens, unfortunately, have become peri-menopausal freeloaders, as they stopped laying eggs at the end of the summer. A real farmer would have brought out the axe and turned them into stewing hens long ago and replaced them with new chicks approaching their reproductive prime. I think it would send the wrong message to the kids about how to treat (argh....) mature women. We didn't acquire any additional livestock species in 2012, although we did evict a very angry opossum that moved into our barn.

We did add three Betta fish to our menagerie. A word to the wise. A $2 fish requires at least $45 of equipment, including a heater since they are native to Thailand, not Upstate NY. There is no economy of scale because they cannot share a bowl...the equivalent exercise would be building a barn for each horse. So, in terms of cost per pet, they are by far our most expensive animals.

As we slip and slide into the real part of winter, it has become much less of an adventure to be stuck on the ice in our own driveway than it was a few years ago. This year we will experiment with winter tires. Although not yet on the car, they're in the garage and I am very happy. It's certainly a step in the right direction.

The final outrage of the year was delivered by our aging (like us) bar-b-cue. Last weekend, after the flame kept dying, Alan lifted the lid and stuck his head in close to try to see the problem (think dim light, bad eyes). And then he hit the ignition. Boom! Repeat of 2006's head full of singed hair, eyelashes and eyebrows. Always the optimist, Alan's reaction was, "Well, at least I have some eyebrows left this time!"

Wishing Your Family a Wonderful Holiday Season!

Alan aka Lord of the Log Splitter, Alyse aka Lady of the Lambs, Jen aka Countess of the Cart, Lil aka Queen of Clay, Zach aka Knight of all Dogs and other critters

Happy Holidays 2013

Well, we did it. In the name of good parenting and in lieu of an XBox, Santa delivered an empty birdcage and a $50 gift certificate to PetsMart. After all, parakeets could never survive a sleigh ride. Already successful chicken-parents, the addition of two 3oz birds (under the care of a highly competent 4th grader) should have been straightforward. Not quite. For those of you who have successfully continued past those little birdies in the window, please note: parakeets are loud. Very. Designed to live in great flocks Down-Under, they add a LOT to our home's background chatter. And because of their communal nature, they pipe-up loudest when Alan's on the phone with work just as a single barking dog inspires a neighborhood chorus. These birds make a pair of roosters seem serene. Also, chickens molt once each year, in the fall, shedding heavy feathers that stay put on the lawn until they blow away...outside. These birds molt continuously, dropping itty bitty feathers so light that the breeze from the heater distributes them throughout the house. You can see them but can't pick them up effectively by hand, with a dustpan, buster or vacuum. It's like swatting flies. Billions of flies. I won't even start with the birdseed. Anyone who knows Alan can imagine the trauma caused by this onslaught of noise, feathers, and birdseed. And as they grew, molting all the way, it became obvious that Pip and Alex were boy and girl and seem to like each other. A lot. We hope the cycle of life doesn't continue in our living room.

To counter Santa's moment of weakness last year, in a demonstration of population control at the Family zoo, we are down to one ram from four. Two are spending the winter in the deep freeze and two moved to Pennsylvania. Enter their replacement: a seven month old ramlamb who will be the end of me. He wouldn't attack as any self-respecting ram might, but he'll trip me by winding around my legs like a cat. So we named him Garfield, and he can't believe his good fortune to be spending December with a dozen lovely ladies who are equally thrilled to spend time with him.

The final, but sad, animal tally is that we are down to one dog after losing Vito to cancer. Fortunately, it was one of those situations that didn't require a gut-wrenching decision on our part and it provided an easy way out for him. We'll always remember Vito for not only having incredibly soft fur, but also for being willing to eat anything. Wanting to expand his pallette from his boring staple of corncobs, sharp bones, candy wrappers and chicken poo, he welcomed spring by barfing up an entire sheep placenta in the dining room.

Time marches on in the kid department, too. Ours have morphed from being incredibly time consuming to being incredibly expensive. In the proverbial blink of an eye we went from micromanaging their bodily functions to dropping Jen off with her skis and a fistful of $20s at the Exit 15 McDonald's to meet her ride for a ski weekend. After that trip, she never saw SkiVenture's outhouse and tattered tow rope the same way again. Her assessment: "I knew SkiVenture was Okie but I had no idea HOW Okie!"

But no matter how grown up they think they are, they still continue to learn lessons. Jen's orthodontist had a "Come-to-Jesus" talk with her and slapped her braces right back on for retainer non-compliance. Once again, let the punishment fit the crime. Horrified at having to explain to her friends why the railroad tracks were back, she couldn't argue as the molds of her newly crooked teeth didn't lie. She also was beyond mortified for passing out in the cubicle with me while I was getting bloodwork done. We'd never heard of that happening to an otherwise healthy spectator but faint she did, rolling out beneath the privacy curtain into the aisle. Did you know that's officially called a "code green?" There was no permanent damage because on the way down Jen's head was cushioned by her giant ponytail, a.k.a. the poof.

Zach is officially in middle school and now wears and can tie his own necktie. Actually, five ties. The first two each lasted only a day and came home beyond repair, disassembled from the knot down. Tie #3 ended up dipped in wet dog food, so we are down to Tie #4 and a backup. Continuing this trek towards adult-hood, the empty swing-set round is now the site of "Zach's House." When Jen caught wind of this birthday plan, she was disgusted. "Are you SERIOUS? NORMAL kids get cell phones or video games and you're getting him a SHED? Like where you put TOOLS?" But it's an adorable shed. Zach loves it and we no longer have to explain the mystery area in our backyard that looked like an abandoned helipad for the last four years.

Lil also continues to evolve. No longer devoted to her yellow blankie, she's transferred her affections to her yellow iPhone. Unexpectedly, this new technology has led to a quieter home since now the most effective way to call the kids to dinner is to send a text. No more yelling upstairs when they're really in the backyard. Verizon finds them anywhere. Lil continues to be the most OSHA-approved family member. Heading out the door for a day with a good friend she announced, "I'm ready to go and I've got my helmet." You never know what might be on the agenda when two 11-year old girls get together in Galway, but it apparently requires head protection.

We're ecstatic to share that Alan and I may have achieved our finest parenting goal, and we're not talking about continuing our family tradition of spreading 40 yards of mulch every Easter Sunday. Drum roll please. We taught the kids to fly to Florida by themselves to visit their grandparents so we could fly somewhere different. We celebrated achieving this Holy Grail of Parenting in Aruba where I was able to read three books in one week and Alan had all the wind he needed in a kiteboarders' paradise. It was perfect until Alan had a technical problem with his kite and started floating quickly in the direction of Venezuela (only 12 miles away) while I watched from our hotel balcony. Thankfully, the water-weenie guy noticed his predicament, took pity on him and hauled him the mile back to the beach.

We hope that this letter finds you all happy and healthy or at least with a good sense of humor. Wishing all of you love and laughter from all of us furry, feathered, finned or otherwise. And as the big day 2013 approaches and Santa warms up his sled, an XBox is still on Zach's wish list along with barn-kitties. We'll let you know how this one pans out, but the other day I did see a mouse dart under the haystack...

Wishing you health and happiness in 2014!

Alan, Alyse, Jen, Lil, Zach

Happy Holidays 2014

2014 began with the early, yet predictable, news from Pat the mail-lady. She'd left her annual note announcing she wasn't coming up our driveway until the ice melted come spring. We understand her trepidation, but then again, FedEx has no problem with the "drive-it-like-you-stole-it" method of getting to our door. However, the note was earlier than expected, as the Fisher luge run isn't usually open for business until the beginning of February.

January also brought some excitement as Lightning the barn cat joined our family under the dual auspices of "Santa Delivery" (in the form of an IOU) and "Rodent Control." The best way to imagine him is in comparison to Weston. If our fussy lab is a cat-dog, then Lightning is a dog-cat. He's orange, long-haired, with a white tuxedo, a raccoon tail and a bunch of extra toes. From a riding-lesson-stable, he'd been manhandled by kids since the day he was born, so he's happiest when carried around upside down like a baby doll or lying flat on his back in the middle of the action, begging for belly rubs. But he harbors a dark side and does his job well as slayer of mice, destroyer of voles and exterminator of birds. But what we didn't anticipate was his taste for baby bunnies. Lightning was thrilled with our bumper crop of rabbits this year, and they were easy to catch since they spent their days frolicking on the lawn.

We drew the line at setting up a bunny hospital to treat the victims. But in order to be at peace with the unpleasant fate of so many of our resident woodland creatures, we ferried rescued rabbits, in various states of disassembly, to the safety of the woods as our summer evening ritual. But most fascinating about this new balance of power was the trophic cascade initiated. Just as reintroducing wolves to Yellowstone allowed aspens to rebound, bringing on Lightning as our apex backyard predator yielded a massive zucchini harvest. In our backyard ecosystem, rabbit destruction translated into zucchini production. We couldn't keep up with the onslaught, and after several months of stuffed, sauteed, grilled and fried, zucchini bread, fritters, frittatas, quiche and pizza crust, the kids hit their wall. It became obvious when still-warm-from-the-garden zuccs, stuffed with lamb sausage and topped with homegrown tomato sauce, were greeted with groans before being flat-out refused. Even suspicious of steak and potatoes, they gave the hairy eyeball to each dinner, "Mom, is zucchini in this?"

But other than the zucchini overload, the kids are doing their thing and are a lot tougher than they let on. We'll never again empathize with their piteous kvetching and gagging while cleaning their own bathroom. This year both Jen and Lil were faced with an "iPhone in the potty" moment. And each girl showed her mettle as they took the plunge without hesitation to make a successful retrieve. But what overshadows their bravery is the obvious question of why their phones were so close to the loo. The real lesson they may or may not have learned is to detach phone from hand once in a while to avoid the heroics entirely.

But to counter these moments of empowerment, Jen's now in high school and enrolled in a crash course of self-acceptance. Since the beginning of time, all teenagers aspire to look like clones, and long straight hair is in vogue at the moment. Jen's facing the reality that while the "long" is possible, the "straight" is not. Not with a capital N. For a 15-year old, it doesn't make a difference that she's regularly stopped on the street by strangers asking if it's real and for permission to touch it. She still considers herself the victim of a genetic mishap. The moral of the story? "Love yourself, because there's a limit to what even the hairdresser can do."

Lil has now joined her sister as a teenager and is appropriately mortified by us. We discovered our new power while we were waiting in the line of cars at school pick-up. She leaped in the car saying "just go Just Go JUST GO!" as if I were driving the get-away car after a bank robbery. "MOM, people are STARING they NOTICE these things...there's a DEAD BAT stuck to the front of the car - WHY ARE YOU LAUGHING IT'S NOT FUNNY!" But it was, and with wings spread like a logo on the front of a comic book, a decent sized bat had taken a header into the center of the decorative grillwork. We still give Lil a hard time for not feeling special, for it isn't every kid who gets picked up in a genuine batmobile! She doesn't get the joke. But she's still the most culinarily gifted person in our family. Taking pride in intricately fondanted cakes, cookies, and truffles, we caught her putting a tower of whipped cream in Weston's dog bowl. Her explanation? "But he hates his food!" So true, but we'd been wondering why 6 months of expensive diet dog food and exercise wasn't yielding results.

On the other end of the epicurian table sits Zach who's proud to have mastered the art of independently preparing "Hungry Man" microwave dinners. Impressed by the fact that pasta, corn, a brownie and fried chicken all come on one tray and cooks in two minutes, he carefully reads the directions, peels the plastic film and he's off. But we're thrilled that he's equally conscientious about schoolwork. This spring he came home reporting the results of his vision test, "My left eye is 1/2 and my right eye is 1/3." It took me a few minutes to realize that even though his eyesight isn't an A+, at least he's reducing his fractions.

As 2014 draws to a close, so does the cycle of the seasons. How can we tell? Our driveway is once again treacherous for any vehicle without 4WD and studded snow tires. We're back on Pat's bad side and are expecting her annual message- she'll see us this spring.

Wishing you health and happiness in 2015

Alan, Alyse, Jen, Lil, Zach, dog, cat, parakeets, chickens, horses, sheep and far fewer yard bunnies

Happy Holidays 2015

The years spent reading storybooks, identifying interesting bugs, and memorizing addresses and phone numbers were abruptly filed in the "nostalgic" folder of our past. Our cortisol levels and resting blood pressures have permanently increased since New York State entrusted Jen with a learner's permit. Our formerly slow, cerebral process of educating our children has become a life or death experience at freeway speeds. For example, in Jen's world, the writing on a speed limit sign means "Get up to that number as fast as possible even from a dead stop, without regard for weather and traffic conditions." Until now, we'd never used or appreciated our car's headrests as whiplash protection. But it's amusing to watch how quickly her teenage bravado dissolves into panic when behind the wheel. And as a parent, it's hard not to be a little smug when "QUIT telling me - I KNOW where I'm going!" is immediately followed at a 4-way stop by "Mom, is it my turn? Get off your phone and HELP me!" or a desperate "WhatdoIdowhatdoIdo?!?" midway around a traffic circle. And it was amazing to watch her tried-and-true "But it was an accident" excuse lose legitimacy when she pulled into the garage and SMACK! Score one for Mom's friendly advice, "Careful, don't hit the golf cart."

For Jen, driving has also become a crash course in local geography. I suspect most teenagers who've grown up in the digital age face the same challenge. They lack 15 years of staring out the window so have no clue where they are or how to get where they're going. As parents, our superpowers of navigation are finally appreciated because WE know how to get home from the grocery store.

In the spirit of developing life skills, we've made forward progress in the "care and feeding" department. Because the females in the house are now roughly the same size, it's impossible to sort laundry accurately. The new rule: You wear it? You wash it. Although Zach still calls the washer the "wetter" (it still sits next to the "dryer"), our laundry routine is nearly under control. Unfortunately, the inside of our dryer resembles a Jackson Pollack painting after being tumbled with permanent Sharpies. Lil continues to lead the charge on the "feeding" front, baking macaroons from scratch and owning her own torch to finish crème brûlée. In predictable contrast, when I asked Zach why he was having granola for a 4th meal in a row, he answered "I'm just not independent enough to feed myself." A few months later, he did master the fine art of microwaving Hot Pockets in their protective cardboard sleeve. Jen just circles around like a shark, trolling for scraps.

Like all middle and high schoolers, the kids are participating in the expected social rituals and are facing the expected complications. Jen managed to rip ALL of the skin off of BOTH of her knees playing indoor lacrosse right before her winter dance thereby ending the conversation about whether the length of the dress (or lack thereof) required tights. Shortly after that debacle, Scott successfully took Lil shoe shopping before her dance. But on the trash day before the big event, he took the suspiciously light shoebox to the curb - new shoes still in it. A surprise to us is that 12-year old Zach is having the easiest time. When I asked him "OK Romeo, what's your secret?" he explained, "Everyone else talks ABOUT the girls, but I talk TO the girls." Sounds good to us.

And since we've finished giving money to the orthodontist, life has mandated that we shift our payments next door to an office with a grown-up clientele. The oral surgeon. Early this year, Zach was freed from an impacted canine, but the injustice of having surgery on a snow day almost tipped him over the edge. Jen followed, kicking off summer vacation by saying adios to her wisdom teeth. Lil's safe for the moment but is waiting to be next in the chair.

Now that the kids are a little older, they've become very helpful with chores and we've discovered the striking difference between boys and girls. When Jen and Lil play the role of farmhand, we dish about the latest gossip. With Zach, the same experience is emotionally exhausting. In one evening alone, I learned strategies to survive a zombie apocalypse, how to use my shepherd's crook as a martial arts weapon, the pay scale for hitmen (kids are cheap and government officials can garner $100K) and, finally, a demonstration of a Ninja roll off of the hood of the golf cart.

Nonetheless, we appreciate family help because our critter total is up 17 from last December, 15 being chickens. Although our older girls were only generating an occasional egg, I'd neglected to order May chickens. So we were wait-listed until we got news of an "overhatch," had our own moment of teenage bravado, and accepted a delivery in early March. Note: This is not a very bright idea unless you live in San Diego. As expected they arrived, a peeping box populated with adorable babies taking up the space of 15 eggs. We loved having them in the living room. For about a week. Here, winter lasts until May and chicks can't take a chill or they'll bite the dust. We'd forgotten that chickens grow really fast and adolescent chickens fly really, really well and their favorite pastimes are scratching and dust-bathing. Our formerly charming nursery morphed into two troughs and two dog crates filled with bored and gawky teenage chickens but still in the living room. They filled their days scratching like crazy in their bedding. This was perfect for our carefully designed open-concept floor plan with fantastic airflow to layer fine particulates over every surface of every corner of the house, both upstairs and down. We still tell Alan it was just "dust from the shavings," but use your imagination. While the dog crates proved effective at chicken containment, the troughs topped by our now-filthy window screens often failed. We'd hear a crash followed by flapping and squawking and chickens were everywhere. Lil was the only one with the patience and agility to catch these maniacs loose in the house. Eventually, we reached the point where we said, "To hell with the birds. They can take their chances outside."

The moral of this story is to be careful what you wish for because by July I was hearing complaints along the lines of "Mom, why do we have 87 eggs in the fridge?" The upside of so many spare eggs was that Beastie, our new "barn cat" who can usually be found in the house, loves to swat them off the counter to the dogs who wait below to lap them off the floor. His partner in crime is Lightning, last years'

baby-rabbit-eater. Lightning (aka Einstein-Cat) has also learned from the dogs how to do tricks for treats (come, sit, leap from chair to chair). However, by the end of winter he'd become so matted we had no choice but to shave him. Einstein-Cat became Embarrassed-Cat after he returned from the vet wearing only boots, a lion's mane and a huge fluffy tail. From a distance he looked exactly like a fox, so we put out an APB so he wouldn't become neighborhood target practice.

And yes, it is once again "dogs." Yul, a yellow guide dog reject joined our pack before Thanksgiving and has been Mr. Perfect except for an occasional litter box snack. Weston also makes poor food choices. For example, Alan included an ember from the fireplace ashes in the kitchen trash

Shortly thereafter, the bag landed behind the garage safely smoldering in the snow. Since we'd eaten chicken the night before, we accepted responsibility for the bellyfull of ashes and chicken drippings Weston barfed in the foyer. He also decided it was an excellent idea to eat more than five pounds of flour from Zach's science project and drooled profusely for days.

But despite the chaos they create, the critters continue to be an endless source of amusement, especially now that we host a complete indoor ecosystem. The cats (predators) relentlessly hunt Zach's parakeets (prey) who taunt them from the safety of their cage. The dogs are the clean-up committee (scavengers). We've concluded that this is our Freudian attempt to use pets as stress relief.

As we consider additional strategies to reduce our blood pressures, we remind ourselves daily that we're the ones who drove Jen to the DMV in the first place, and we signed the "ok to drive" piece of paper. Even so, we're thankful she has an iPhone so Siri can direct her home... but only if we did a good job as parents and she can remember her address.

Wishing you all a fantastic 2016!

Alan, Alyse, Jen, Lil, Zach, Horses, Sheep, Chickens, Dogs, Cats and Parakeets

Happy Holidays 2016

20th Edition (Yes, we've been subjecting you to this for that long.)

One snowy day in January, Jen (16) and Zach (12) were abandoned at the kitchen island under orders to snack and start homework while I collected Lil from the late bus. Upon return, I was greeted with the following grievance, "Mom, did you hear what she did? She hit me with a piece of turkey. So I took the juice and rubbed it in her hair. Then she kicked me. When I get bigger I'm gonna kick her a**!" All I could muster was "okay." This interaction was both disturbing and symbolic. Disturbing, because of the assumption I could hear this violent interaction via mom-omniscience during my peaceful one-kid drive. Symbolic, because as all parents, we dream that our progeny will like each other. That way, when we're dead and gone, they'll provide enough mutual support so our tribe can continue. Clearly, we are not there.

2016 was a year illustrating that life at our farm reads like a script of a Disney movie. As time passes, the characters and their circumstances evolve, but the themes? Absolutely the same. Over and over again. We are a predictable people. Other than Weston greeting us at the door with a heating grate dangling from his collar, nothing seemed particularly out of character.

Sibling harmony continued in the girls' Jack-and-Jill bathroom, constructed at considerable expense to foster their independence and privacy. Not aspiring to HGTV perfection, we let nature take its course, a la Lord of the Flies. The problem is that these are two radically different girls. Jen continues living by frat-house standards while Lil remains a Type-A hoarder. Their two main sources of contention are the two common drains. Ongoing warfare rages about what should trigger a hair-trap cleanout as Jen's only motivated when the water reaches mid-calf by mid-shower. The other question requiring formal mediation or a tribunal is "By whom and when does the potty need to be plunged? Is it the immediate responsibility of the clogger, or is that responsibility transferred to the last knowingly post-clog user?" That, dear friends and family, IS the question debated with raised voices and red faces in our home this year. More than once.

Although we've long accepted their differences, it's still surprising how consistent each is over time. We revisited the scene of last year's June ritual - packing for sleepaway camp. Less than a day before departure, Lil's trunk looked like a flagship GAP store and because of the folding job, it weighed in at least 400lbs. Zach's room looked like an IED exploded in his closet, while his trunk was still empty. Armed with the authority of THE LIST ("It says you need 14 pairs of socks, now go find 11 more!") we managed to pack him while he feigned exhaustion on the floor. As expected, evidenced by pictures posted online, not ONCE was Lil wearing her own clothes and Zach arrived home with quite a few more socks than he packed... so if anyone is missing their children's socks, please let us know.

It's not just the kids who generate repeat performances. Alan, always the promoter of efficiency and speed, attempted to cook bacon in the oven. Not crisping quickly enough, he directed Lil to turn on the broiler as he left the house. It was a simple recipe because the ingredients for a grease fire are 1.) Grease and 2.) Fire. In our case, it was top-rack bacon and a gas broiler. Racing home to a smoky kitchen, he ran the flaming bacon into the snow, spattering the breezeway as he went. For months afterwards, the dogs wouldn't go out except to lick their tongues raw on the spatter-infused concrete. In keeping with dog logic, "If it smells this good, there's gotta be bacon in there somewhere." But I will admit that bacon smoke smells a whole lot better than Alan's spontaneously combusted linseed oil

(2001) and didn't require a visit to the barber for emergency burnt eyelash and hair trims (2006, 2011). Look out 2021!

As a group, we continue our mission of appliance destruction. While it's easy to write off six dead vacuum cleaners in a decade to the pressure of pet hair and hay tracked from the barn, it's harder to explain the graveyard of microwaves, coffeemakers, blenders, washing machine, mixer, and a dishwasher saved "for parts." This year we even did in a toaster. Shocked, we thought toasters lived forever. Everyone acquires one with their first apartment, and then upon death, nobody wants it because they already have one that works. But I know we're resigned to this pattern because while replacing our 2nd microwave in two years, I asked Alan, "Do you want to keep the turntable?" His straight-faced answer, "We usually do," was subtle, yet telling.

While we adults focused on appliances, our kids branched out into destroying screens, specifically four iPhones and one laptop. It's amazing how resourceful they are with packing tape when the alternative is handing over $100+ and their phone to the shady guy at the iFixit kiosk at the mall.

And we're still playing the role of tech support for my folks. While their goals stay ambitious, their execution remains poor. We thought it would be helpful to introduce them to the magic of voice control - FAIL. Their "pleases," "thank yous" and mid-command equivocation caused Siri a complete meltdown. As Lil found out, Siri doesn't deal well with ambiguity. Midway through class a confused Siri piped up, "I didn't quite get that, SexyBitch."

As time marches on, we are accepting the reality of our predictable story and are beginning to take comfort in its consistency. It's why two of our kids rushed out to see Moana, afterwards proclaiming it the best movie ever. Even as self-declared adults, they like knowing how stories end. So as 2016 draws to a close, as expected, Alan's saved most of his vacation for December to take advantage of snow-themed family fun. Of course, there is no snow...yet.

Wishing you the absolute best in 2017!

Love, Alan, Alyse, Jen, Lil, Zach & 49 assorted creatures

Happy Holidays 2017

Our Barn Cat Project, originating in the winter of 2015, was unexpectedly popular with everyone except the mice. The irony was not lost on us that out of our 43 creatures, the kids' overwhelming favorite is the free cat (formerly cats). Unfortunately, our resident coyotes were equally enthusiastic about them and then there was one. The kids demanded we protect Lightning at all costs, so now he's inside for good. But indoor cats require indoor kitty litter, and therein lies the rub.

We recently caved and signed up for Amazon Prime because of its miracle promise of free 2-day delivery. Our kids are in constant and legitimate need of random things on short notice. It's impossible to find silver metallic stretch pants or unflavored chewing gum in our neck of the woods, especially on a deadline. And since we joined, Amazon Prime has successfully eliminated most of our scavenger hunts. Alan in particular is thrilled by being able to order "parts," which have become a significant family budget line-item. Most recently, a 44" Magnesium Anode rod for the water heater, a set of golf cart tires, and a 3000 psi pressure washer pump were delivered swiftly and gratis. But even more amazing was finding the "Prime" logo next to a 40lb, $8 box of cat litter - SCORE! The first box arrived flawlessly and I was appropriately smug for having discovered this key to the universe. But the jig was soon up. Apparently, we're not the only ones who consider this service essential to life. Because of its popularity, Amazon began using the USPS for deliveries in our area. We've always accepted our postperson's "Icy Driveway. Come pick up your package." notes as legitimate safety concerns. But now, on a fine spring day, VERY HEAVY appeared in the comment section of our mailbox note, all caps and underlined. No s***, Sherlock. The "Very Heavy" is why I hit "Place Order."

As economic theory predicts, private companies would tolerate none of this nonsense. In January, we were surprised when our doorbell didn't trigger the dog-early-warning/response-system. It turned out to be an Upstate NY remake of "Castaway," and on our front porch stood a miserable FedEx driver, snow packed to his knees, no truck in sight, clutching a box. Our scene ended with Alan driving his tractor down the driveway with the FedEx guy balanced on the tender, gripping a set of tow straps, ready to be pulled out of our culvert so he could continue his route. This effort paled in comparison to the UPS driver who, a few years ago, risked life, limb, and his semi, on glare ice to deliver a full-sized air hockey table on December 23rd. He also required tractor and tow straps to leave our driveway. Clearly, Amazon has to iron out a few things with the USPS, but for now the question remains, "When choosing a shipping company, to which Rudolph would you hook your sleigh?"

In addition to this lesson about economic incentives, having Lightning on permanent lockdown has been eye-opening. While dogs and parakeets maintain roughly our sleep/wake schedule, living with a nocturnal predator with retractable claws is unnerving. After spending the day sound asleep, night falls and Lightning is ready for action. Relentlessly hunting moving feet and dangling pajama-bottom ties, he's waiting, wide-eyed, should you wake up for any reason. The other thing that Lightning added to our home was cat fur. We knew he was hairy but didn't realize that his fur was the mammalian equivalent to parakeet feathers, so light and fine that when the light is right you can see tufts of orange fluff float by at eye level. The obvious solution was my Mother's Day present from years ago, a stainless steel and orange shop-vac. Pressed into service on a daily basis, it's become a permanent resident of our living room. It was so effective we invested in enough hose extensions to reach every crevice from one central location. We decide our redneck central vac will remain since we've long given up any aspirations to live in a house that looks like it's staged.

The kids continue evolving and for the moment all three are impressively within +/- 5% of each other in both height and weight. One big change was Jen's metamorphosis into a full-fledged driver. Previously a foot-dragging sloth complaining about how she's always early to the bus stop, she's now driving Lil and Zach to school and that's triggered a mom-mode we did not anticipate. Every morning she's ready at least 20 min early, announces the departure time well in advance, threatens to leave Zach if he's not in the car on time, complains about the unpredictability of rush hour traffic, bitches about trash left in the car, and completes a countdown a la NASA (4 minutes, 3 minute, 2 minutes, quick threat, get in the car NOW!). Meanwhile, Lil and Zach enter full kid-mode, countering with "It's not called traffic when five cars pass you", "You know that when we get to school there's only three cars in the parking lot", "When I can drive we're leaving at 6:45 like all the NORMAL people." Even bagels and Goldfish are banned because of the "orange powder" and the balled-up foil left stuffed between seats. Then with a jingle of keys, they're off... but not really as we track their iPhones with our own.

As the only kid still on the growth curve, Zach continues to keep us on our toes. This summer, Alan warned him to be careful when cutting spare ribs with a butcher knife. His response, "Don't worry. I'm an international assassin and I took pit cooking at camp." And it's a good thing he's growing so fast because he grows out of his clothes before he has time to destroy them. One exception was his new school wingtips. The tongue "fell out." I'm not sure if this is a common male problem, but the mystery was the stains. "I tried to fix it with Gorilla Glue." Of course. We'll definitely be crossing off "cobbler" as a potential career. But in his defense, Zach is trainable. A yell upstairs, "Zach, it's your day to close the chicken coop!" yielded a reflexive response. He showed up dressed for school in Lil's room, to be met with a snarky comment about it being an unfunny joke. It took him a solid minute to wake up enough to realize it was 7PM on a Saturday night. It's good to know that a holler upstairs means wake up and put on your uniform.

Lil remains the Queen of our Kitchen, turning pumpkin scones and lemon meringue pies into art. We can't help but be sympathetic that she has to live with barbarians like us. A recent breakfast request was, "Eggs with cheese, but could the cheese not be moldy... pleeease?" With an eye to design, she plates her snacks, accessories her room according to season and contours her face. Her notable failure this year was an attempt to add a tropical touch to her room with a hermit crab. While shopping with Floridian grandparents, she got suckered into "Buy the clear tub with plastic palm tree and get the crab free." When she fessed up over the phone, it initially sounded okay. As evidenced by our backyard, I'm not against collecting animals, and as a kid I remember having hermit crabs in Houston without incident. Zone 9. A quick WikiHow revealed that this tropical transplant would require a tropical habitat,

a friend, and an expensive heated and humidity controlled crabitat. Minimum, 150 bucks. And a little more research revealed you can't bring a hermit crab in a cage on a plane like a Yorkie in a carrier. She abandoned the poor creature, likely poached from the wild and trafficked through fancy St. Armand's Circle, in the care of a local reptile rescue.

But Lil isn't the only one showcasing kitchen creativity. Alan issues a daily challenge when he visits the basement freezers each morning with the assignment "Bring something up for dinner." Because we either raise our own or buy by the animal, what ends up defrosting in our sink each morning is always a surprise. Each night is a real life episode of the "Chopped" cooking show. For dinner, the challenge could be to incorporate a smoked ham hock and three pounds of stew meat, or to whip up something with a lamb liver and some breakfast sausage links. Needless to say, we've gotten some raised eyebrows from the kids' friends who dare join us for dinner. But no matter what the result, even the "fails" get eaten by the dogs, chickens, or cats. Yes, cats. We thought we'd reached a rodent equilibrium when Lightning's responsibility in the barn was adopted by a very, very fat snake that seemed to be doing his job. Then one day, a very hungry orange kitty took up residence in the haystack. Although we can't touch him yet, he makes a nightly appearance to claim a bowl of cat food and "scraps of the day." The kids, of course, continue squabbling over his name, Bolt vs. Cashew. However, it might be a moot point as we're not 100% sure he doesn't belong to the neighbors anyway.

Wishing your family a wonderful 2018!
Alan, Alyse, Jen (18), Lil (16), Zach (14) & the other 43

Acknowledgments

Thanks to our daughter, Alisa Fisher, I've learned appreciation for the beauty and power of the land, the incredible nature of animals, and the fun and heartbreak of participating in a farming life. I believe I've become a more forgiving mother and a less judgmental human being enlightened in so many ways by being the mother of a farmer. It has not always been easy, but I'm lucky beyond my wildest dreams to have accidentally become the Mother of this particular Daughter.

I also recognize our son-in-law, Scott, and their children, my grandchildren. They've done more than their share of hard work.

Thanks to Kaylee Fisher for creating the publisher imprint, *Tomatoes In Sunflower Basket*.

Thanks to Cheryl Tomas for her dedication to this work.

Thanks to Austin Metze who designed the cover that speaks both to the simplicity and the complexity of farm life.

The cover photo is from the IcyAcres photo archives.

I am grateful to my advance readers, Joyce Radochia, Judith Leader, Joyce Robinson and Dianne Cooper.

Finally, I am grateful to my husband, Ralph M. Warrington, 3rd, the Father of this Daughter. His patience has been essential.

Freda S. Warrington
www.fredaSwarrington.com

All profits from this work are donated to research for multiple sclerosis.

Biography

Freda Spector Warrington grew up in Arlington, Massachusetts. She received her bachelor's degree from Vassar College and then studied library science at Simmons, education at Tulane and LSU, and counseling at Cal State University, Bakersfield. She was an editor, a public school teacher and a piano instructor who later spent the majority of her career in the healthcare field.

She was in charge of outpatient addiction recovery programs in a psychiatric hospital clinic and served as executive director of Healthy Mothers, Healthy Babies of Kern County, a collaborative organization that addressed high infant mortality and morbidity in California's Central Valley. She also was project director for a federal CSAP collaborative grant for Kern County and worked as a consultant for California Women's Commission on Addictions providing trainings and technical assistance both in Kern and Orange Counties. She was past President of Orange Coast Interfaith Shelter's Friends Board and a representative for seven central California counties to the Governor's task force on addiction. She also supervised substance abuse treatment programs for Native Americans and for people with developmental disabilities.

Freda is married to Ralph Warrington, a retired project manager for Shell Oil company. They have two children and six grandchildren.

For further information, please go to: www.fredaSwarrington.com

Made in the USA
Middletown, DE
03 August 2018